Copyright Marilyn Henrion 2018
ISBN-13: 978-1717570611
ISBN-10: 1717570615

All rights reserved
marilynhenrion@mac.com.   www.marilynhenrion.com
Published by thesohobookie.com

Photography; Jean Vong

NEW ORLEANS REVISITED

new works by

MARILYN HENRION

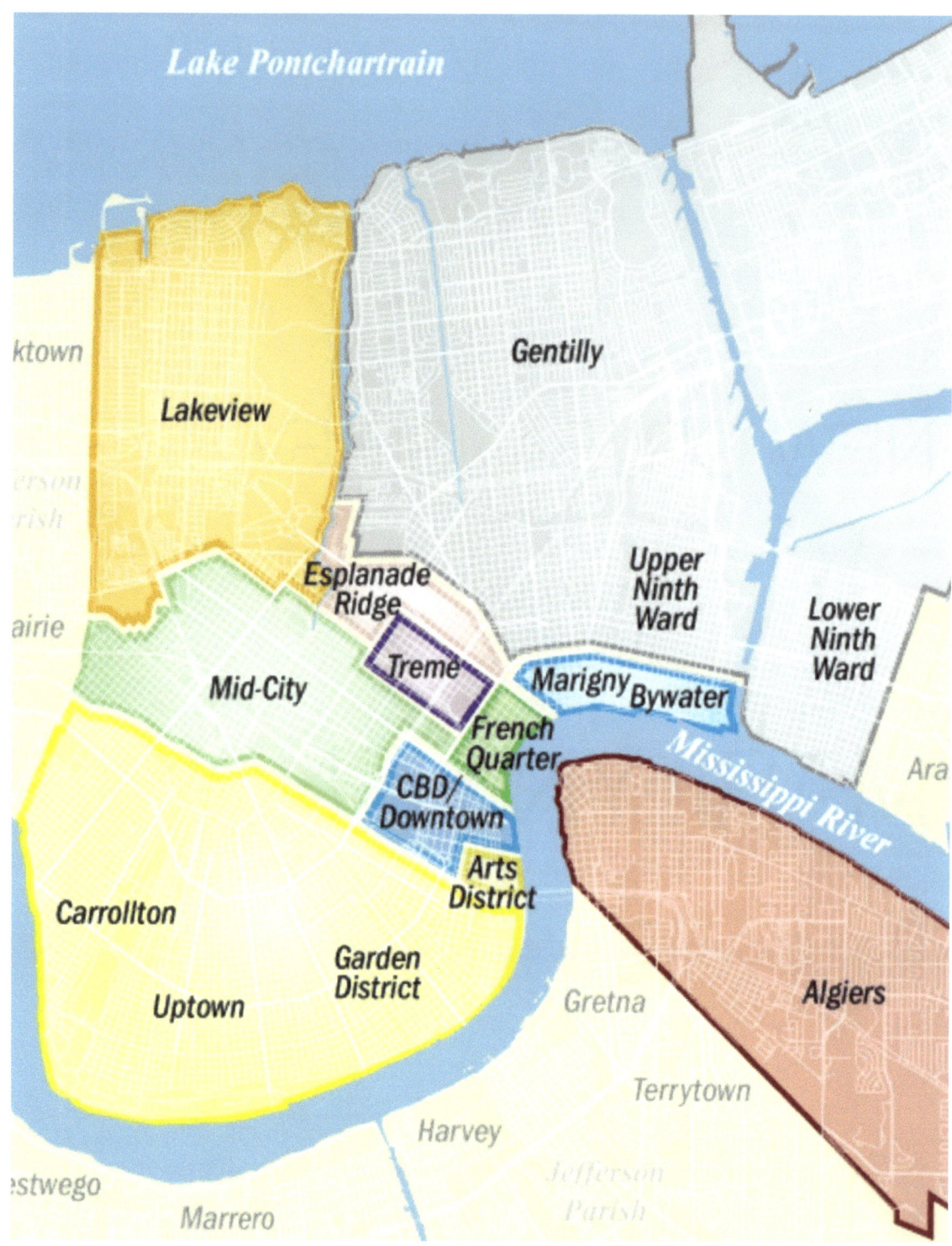

New Orleans Neighborhoods

INTRODUCTION

In 2017, I was in New Orleans in conjunction with an exhibition of my work at the Jonathan Ferrara Gallery. Fifty years since my last visit in the 1960's. I found a vibrant city that had survived the harshest devastation of nature in the form of hurricane Katrina in 2010…..not only survived, but audaciously so, with all the color and sassiness imaginable. With the most generous Southern hospitality of my host, Bee Fitzpatrick, a New Orleans native to whom I am most grateful, I had the opportunity not only to become reacquainted with the streets of the Garden District and the French Quarter which had lingered in my memory, but to become introduced to hitherto unexplored neighborhoods such as Marigny and Bywater.

My camera recorded the images which were later digitally manipulated in my computer and printed onto fabric. The resulting series includes linen collages as well as hand-quilted works on cotton. The concentric circles of the hand quilting patterns echo the ripples of water that are left in memory only. The quotations that are interspersed with the images reflect the impact that this city has had on artists for generations and no doubt will have for generations to come.

Marilyn Henrion, New York City, 2018

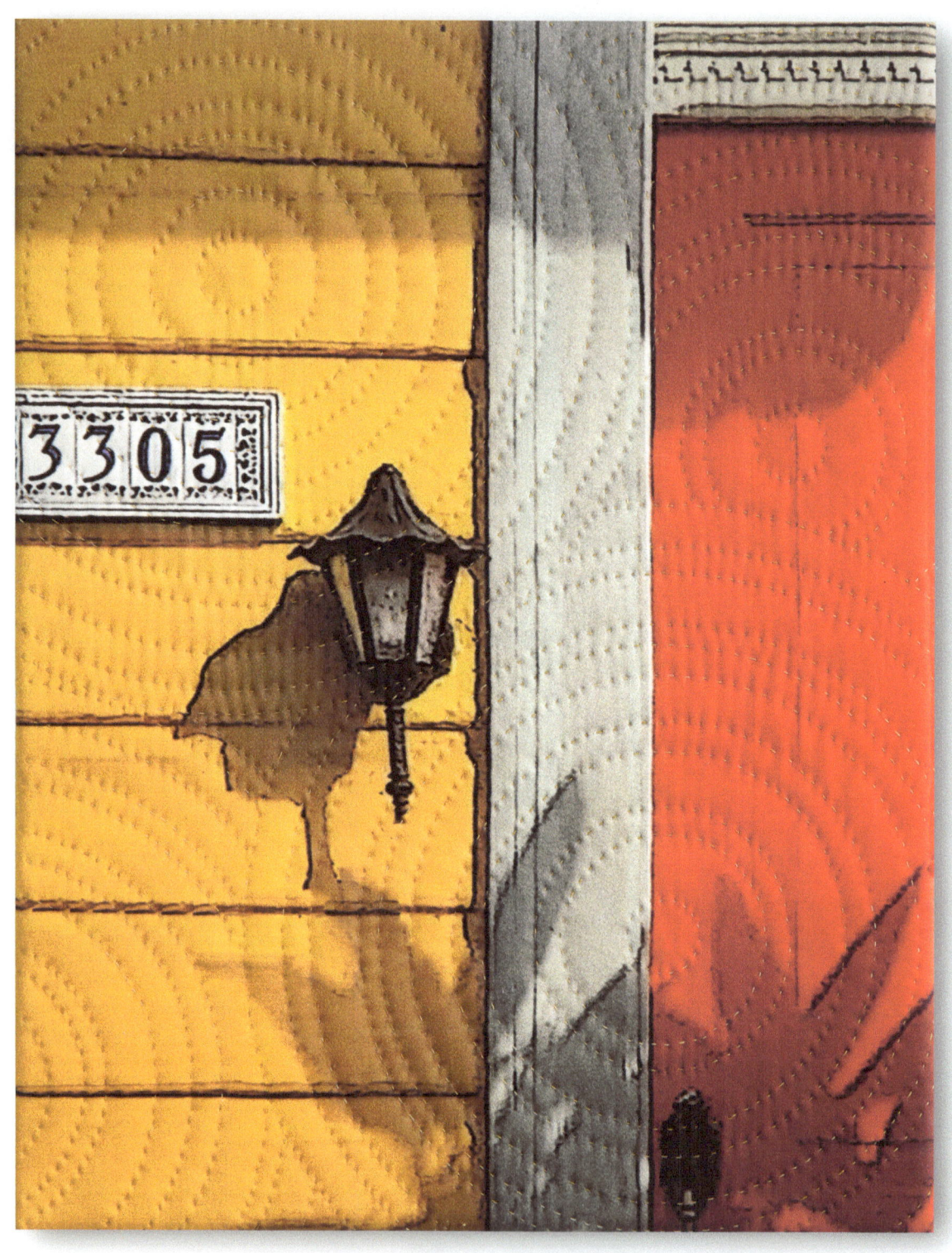

Chestnut Street 14"x11". cotton, hand quilted

A Traveler in Marilyn Henrion's New Orleans

An Essay by Ed Wetschler

No sooner does someone write or speak those two magic words -- New Orleans -- than the rest of us conjure up an image of Bourbon Street, with its old brick facades and iron railings. The next image that pops up in our heads may be Mardi Gras celebrants, or musicians in straw hats playing Dixieland jazz, or a bowlful of jambalaya with sausage and spicy prawns. Or maybe we picture a streetcar in the mansion-lined Garden District. Or the horrors of Hurricane Katrina.

Those are the typical associations, but one of Marilyn Henrion's many gifts is that she has never felt compelled to show you what you already see. It's a quality that has inspired museums, private collectors, corporations, and nonprofits from New York City to the U.S. State Department, from Cambodia to Lebanon, to acquire her work. Over the years these works have explored abstract, urban, and natural themes (and only occasionally the human face), but whatever the theme, Henrion has always revealed subtle truths that we wouldn't otherwise have noticed. Her works illuminate relationships -- shapes, colors, textures -- in ways that immediately strike the viewer as "right," no matter how abstract or how representational. And so it is with this "New Orleans Revisited" series.

For example, "Pleasant Street" (p.11) and "First Street" (p.19) had their geneses when Henrion took photos while exploring the city in 2017. "I cropped these photos, then cropped more and more again until I got to the essence," says Henrion. Thus, instead of the typical long views of brick buildings sporting wrought iron balconies or of Garden District mansions with their ornamental wrought iron railings, Henrion focused on the shapes and the beauty of the details. She then manipulated the photos on her computer, printed them onto cotton fabric, and hand-quilted the fabric with concentric circles representing, as she puts it, "ripples of water that are left in memory only."

I first visited New Orleans as a novice travel writer in the 1980s, and I do not recall its buildings as having been as colorful then as they are today. Henrion has similar memories. "New Orleans wasn't what I'd expected," she says of her first visit. "I remember grand mansions, but not much color." When she returned in 2017 for an exhibition featuring some of her work, though, she was struck by the bright hues with which "urban pioneers" had freshened up old buildings. Were these historically accurate colors? Not necessarily, yet these bold hues are nonetheless appropriate, because N'Awlins is and always has been nothing if not bold. Henrion gets it, and she helps you get it, as well.

For example "Chartres Street" (p.13) proves for all time that a red door, slate-blue shutters, and yellow clapboard -- a combination that might drive your neighbors crazy if you used it in Westchester or San Diego or the suburbs of Atlanta -- is never too much in The Big Easy. Similarly, in "St. Ferdinand Street" (p.5) Henrion draws our attention to a powder-blue facade with green shutters framed by crimson molding. Yes, that's a lot of color for the front of one house. Moreover, these are not the tastefully dark green shutters that adorn homes in other cities; these shutters are dressed in a bright, almost electric green. "It isn't easy being green," said Kermit, but it is in New Orleans. Another thing that holds your attention in this and other works: The colors seem to highlight Henrion's stitching, those circular "ripples of water" that nurture and threaten this building and, really, all of New Orleans.

In addition to being what may be the most colorful (figuratively as well as literally) city in the USA, this is also a sultry, southern town, a place where you're grateful for the shade of ancient live oaks and magnolias in the heat of the day. In "Spain Street" (p.15) and the three "Marigny Street" pieces (p. 23, 26, 28), those trees cast dappled shadows on tan, teal, and purple walls. The shadows have such presence in these works that they convey the essence of trees without the viewer even seeing a single tree.

The three NOLA Gumbo works in this series (p. 31, 32, 33) almost -- but only almost -- seem to belong to another series altogether. Instead of being stitched, quilt-like fabrics, these are linen collages that recombine Henrion's impressions of the city in ways that heighten its shapes, intricate details, and bawdy hues. This is the first time in Henrion's ever-evolving path as an artist that she has taken two such different approaches toward her subject within one series. These two approaches, though, serve the same goal, and that's a goal she has pursued in her native New York and in places as far-flung as Moscow and Kyoto: to illustrate what she calls "the geometry of the city." Nobody does it better, and for bonus points her approach illuminates the very souls of cities. She closes in on the minutiae that matter, and she deconstructs and rearranges each city's architecture and bones until its essence is revealed and its reality heightened. What's old seems new again, and that is the quality and the power of "New Orleans Revisited."

Ed Wetschler, a contributing editor at Recommend magazine, is a veteran travel writer for whom the art of/about a destination is the key to its character.

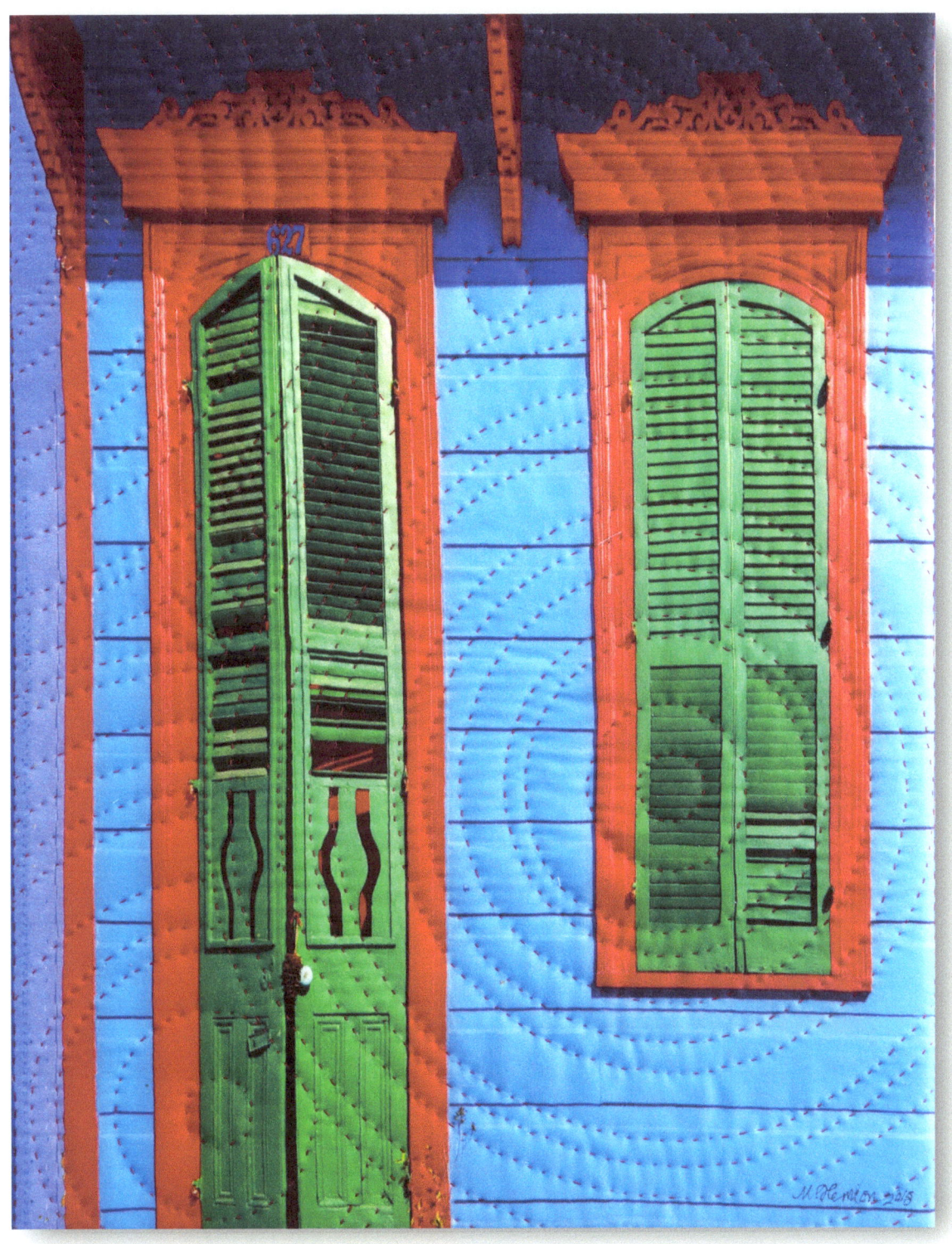

St. Ferdinand Street   14"x11".   cotton, hand quilted

"America has only three cities: New York, San Francisco, and New Orleans. Everywhere else is Cleveland."

—Tennessee Williams

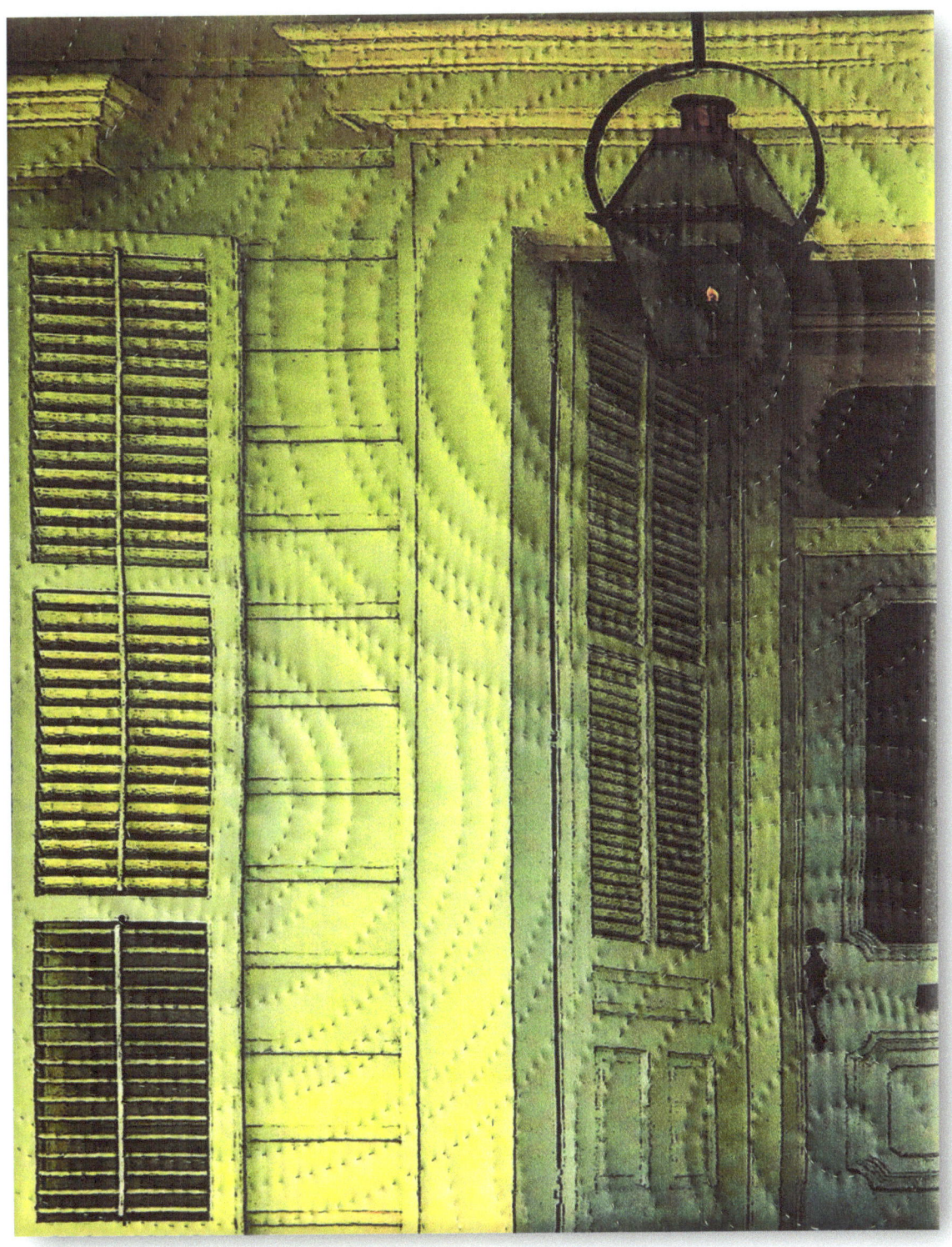

Philip Street   14"x11".   cotton, hand quilted

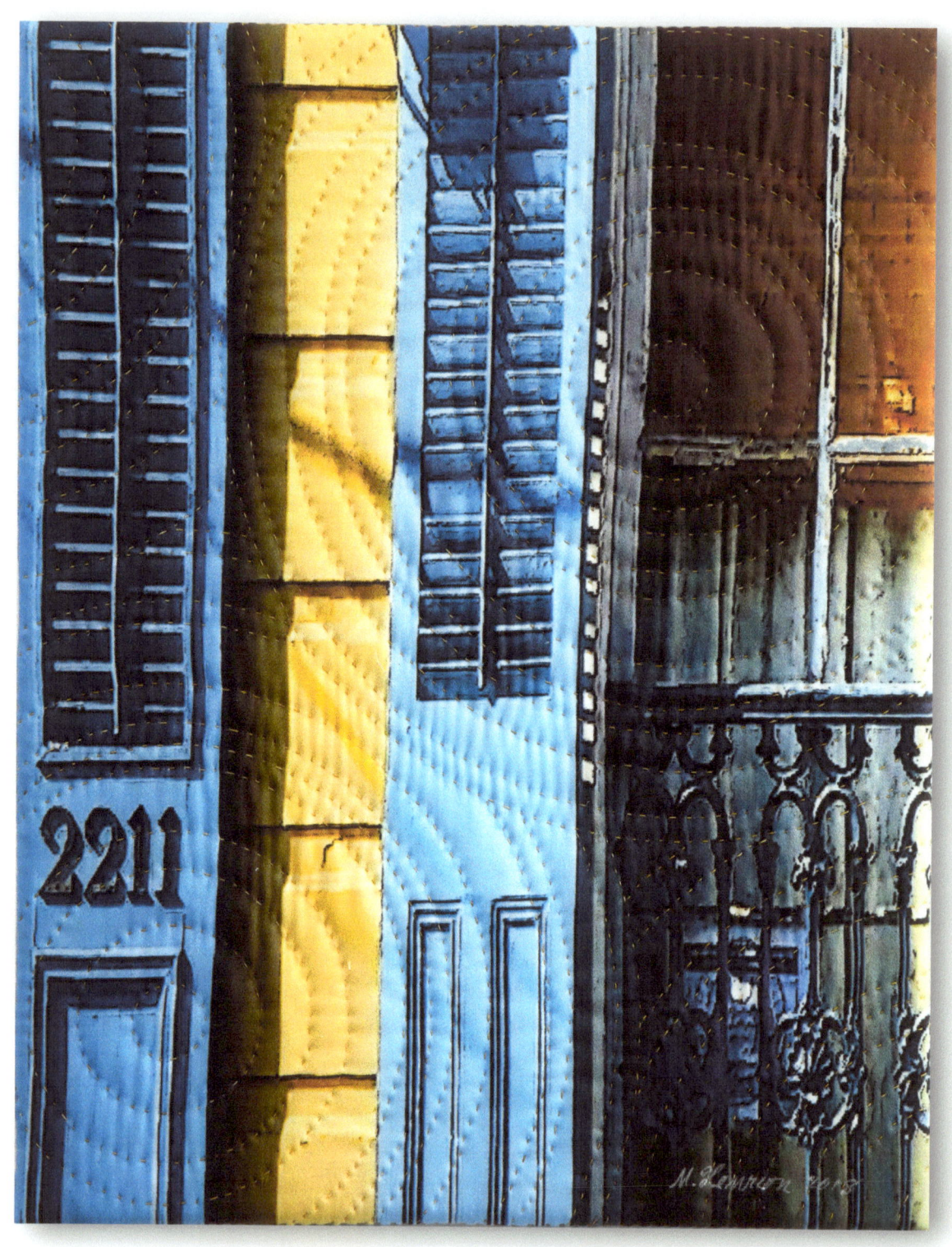

Chartres Street 2   14"x11".   cotton, hand quilted

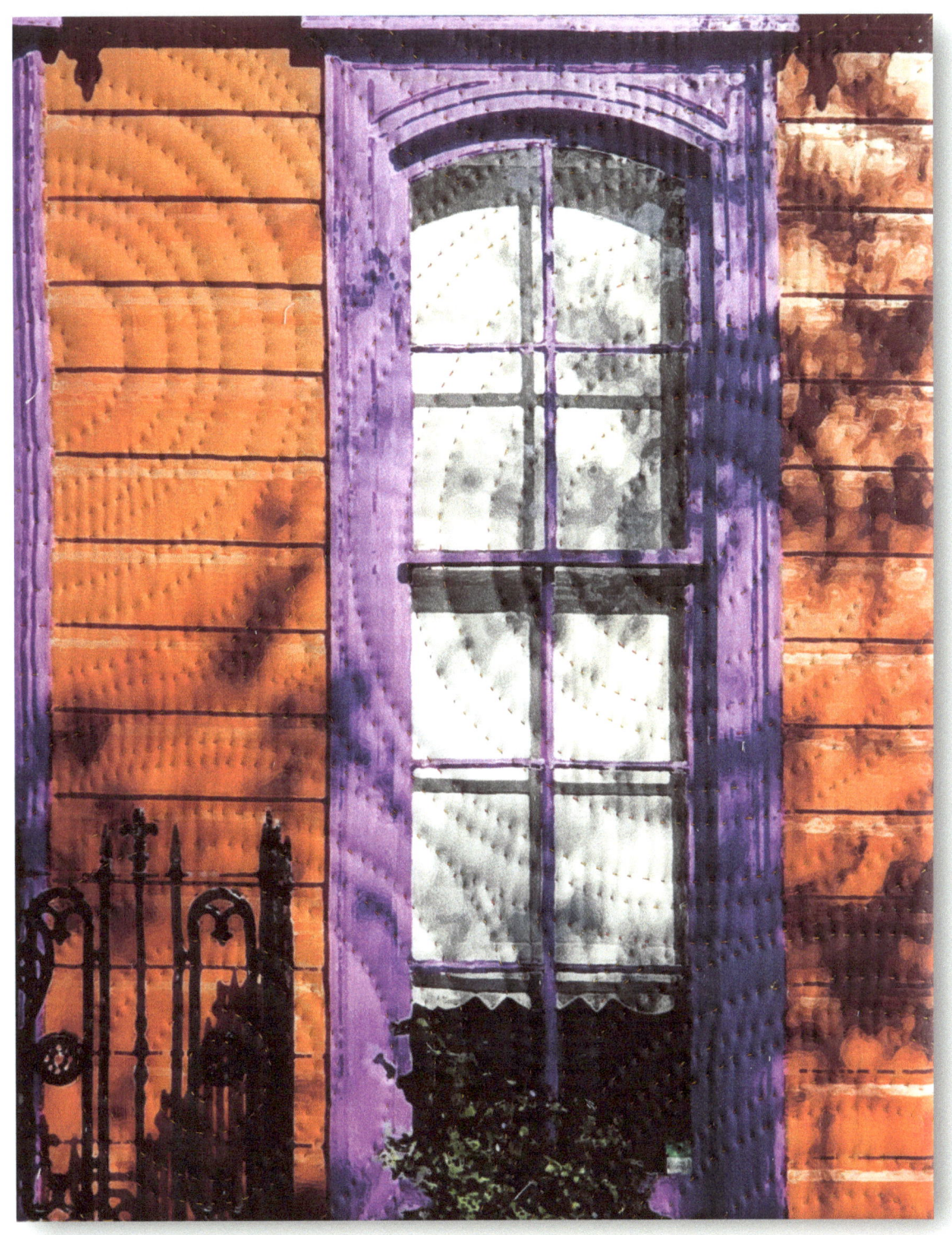

Mandeville Street   14"x11".   cotton, hand quilted

"Somewhere between Preservation Hall and the Superdome, between voodoo and cybernetics, New Orleans listens eagerly to the seductive promises of the future but keeps at least one foot firmly planted in its history, and in the end, conforms, like an artist, not to the world but to its own inner being–ever mindful of its personal style."

– Tom Robbins, Jitterbug Perfume, 1984

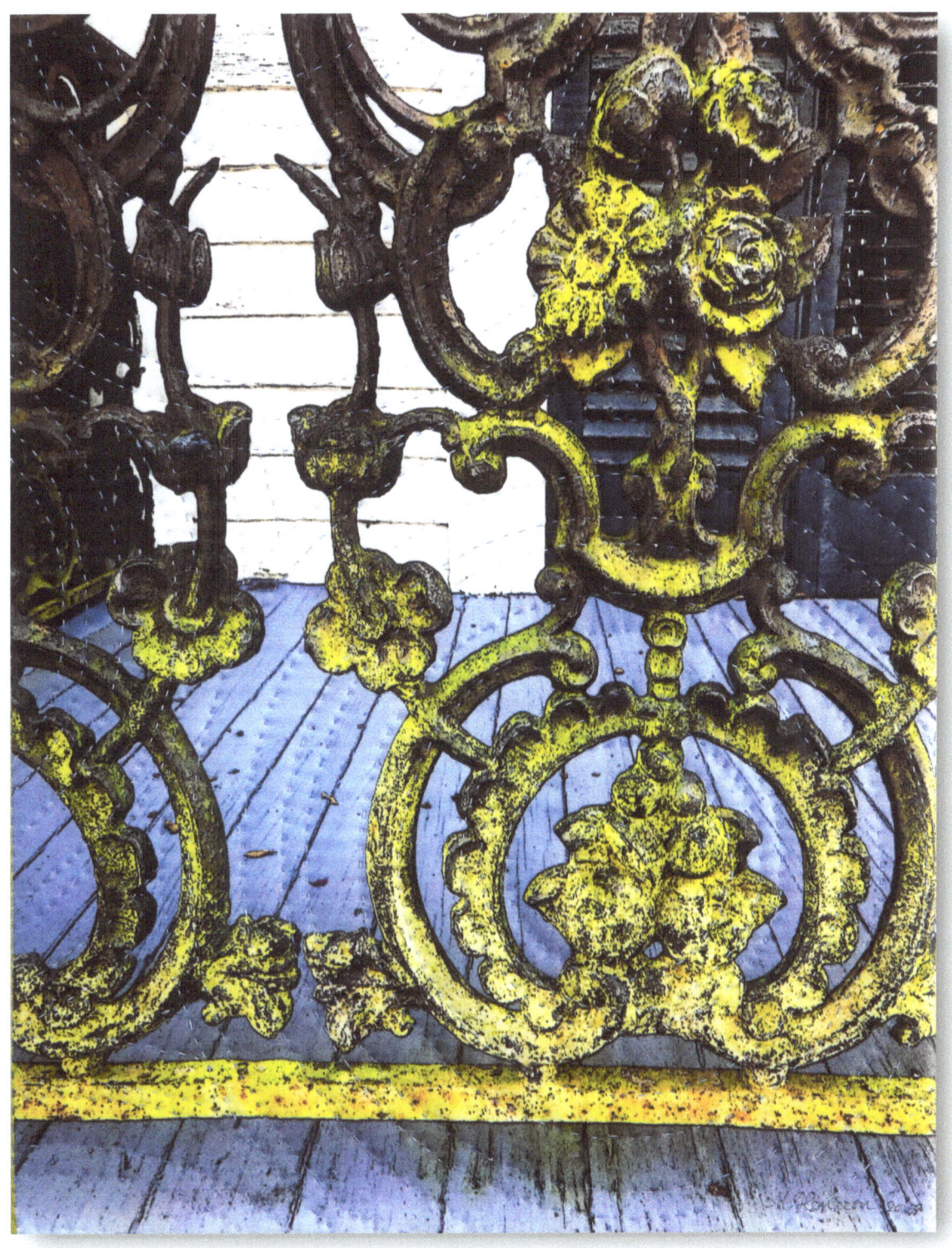

Pleasant Street   14"x11".   cotton, hand quilted

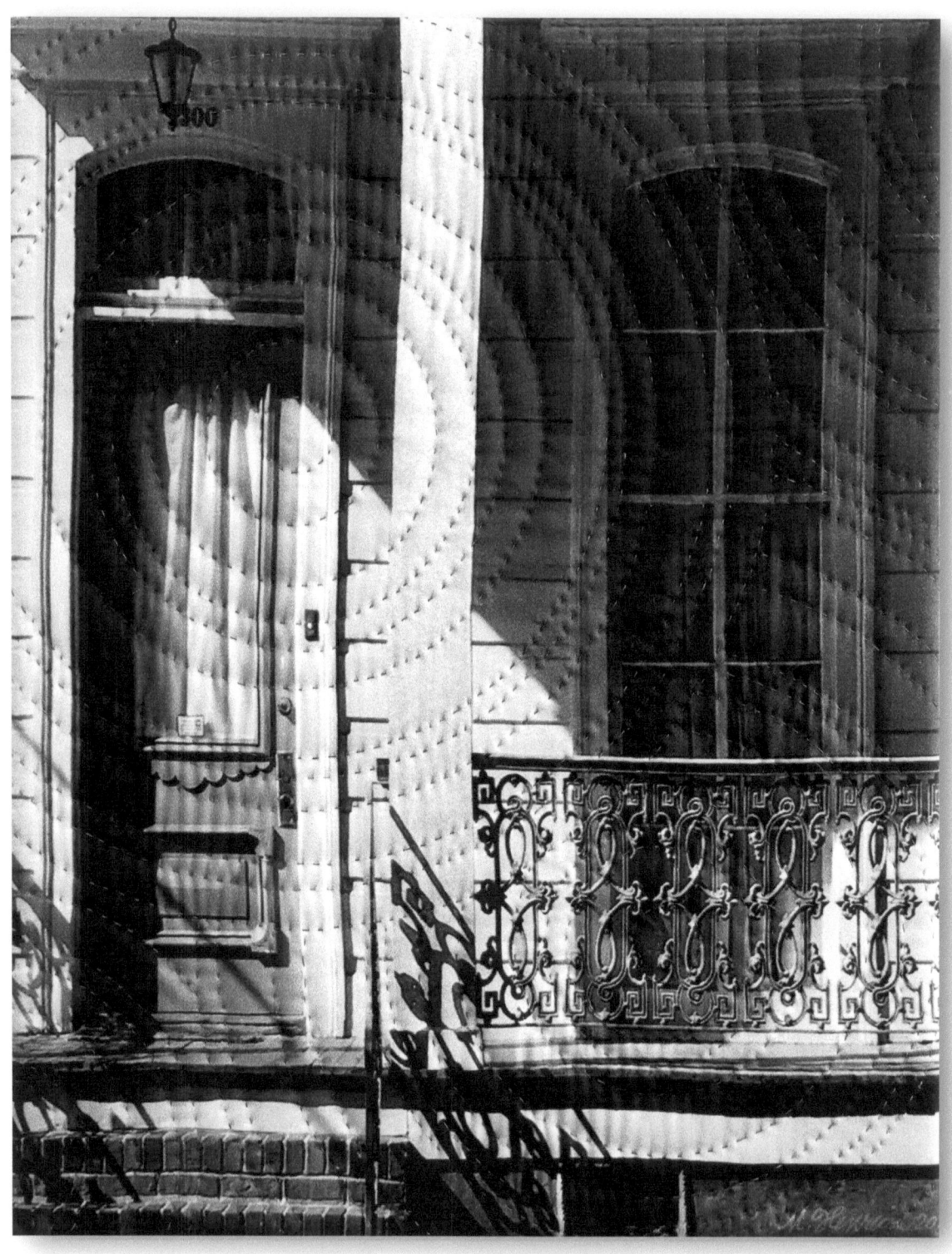

Seventh Street   14"x11".   cotton, hand quilted

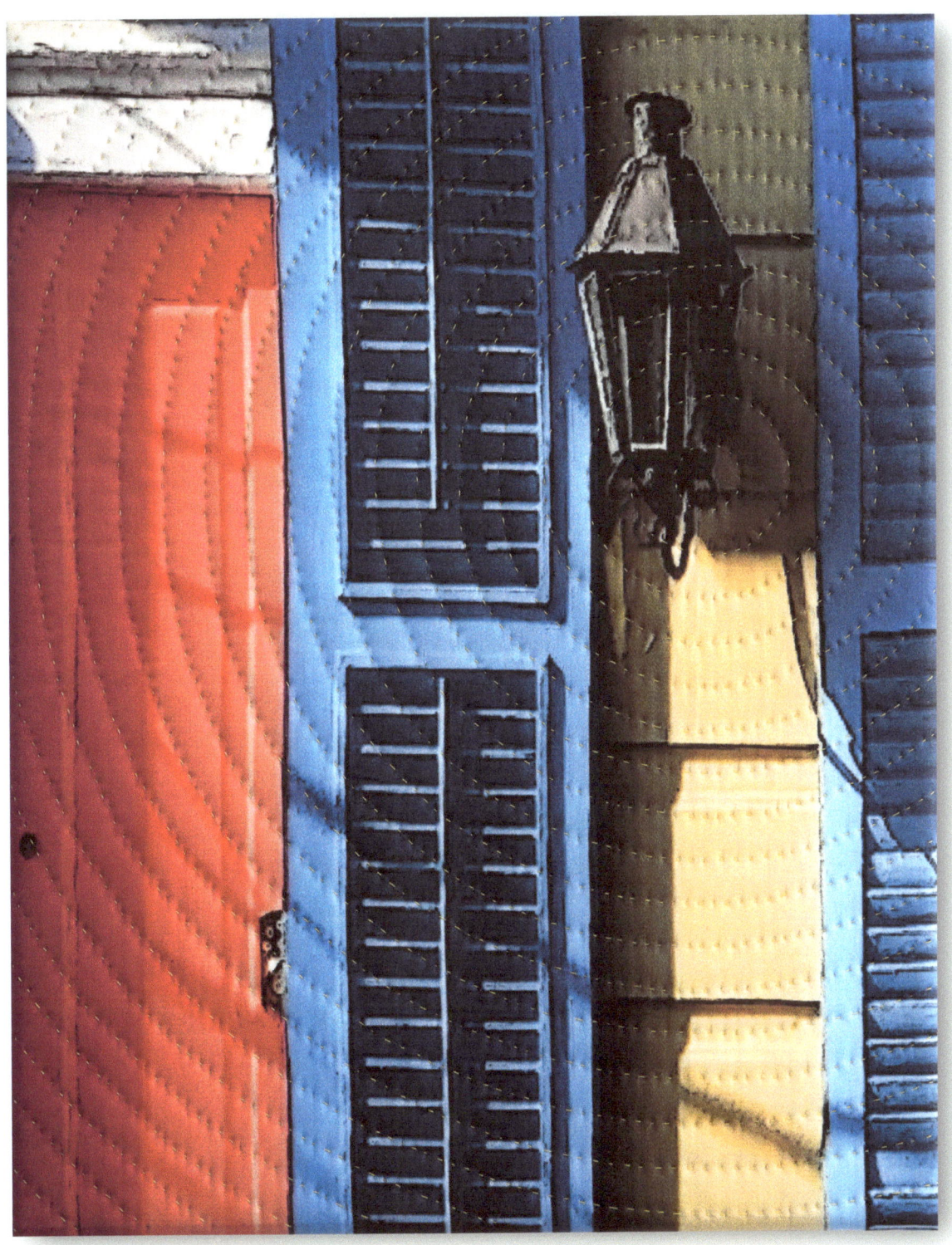

Chartres Street   14"x11".   cotton, hand quilted

"The morning sun in New Orleans felt like it was trying to make a point, convincing the old world to believe something new."

— Hunter Murphy, Imogene in New Orleans

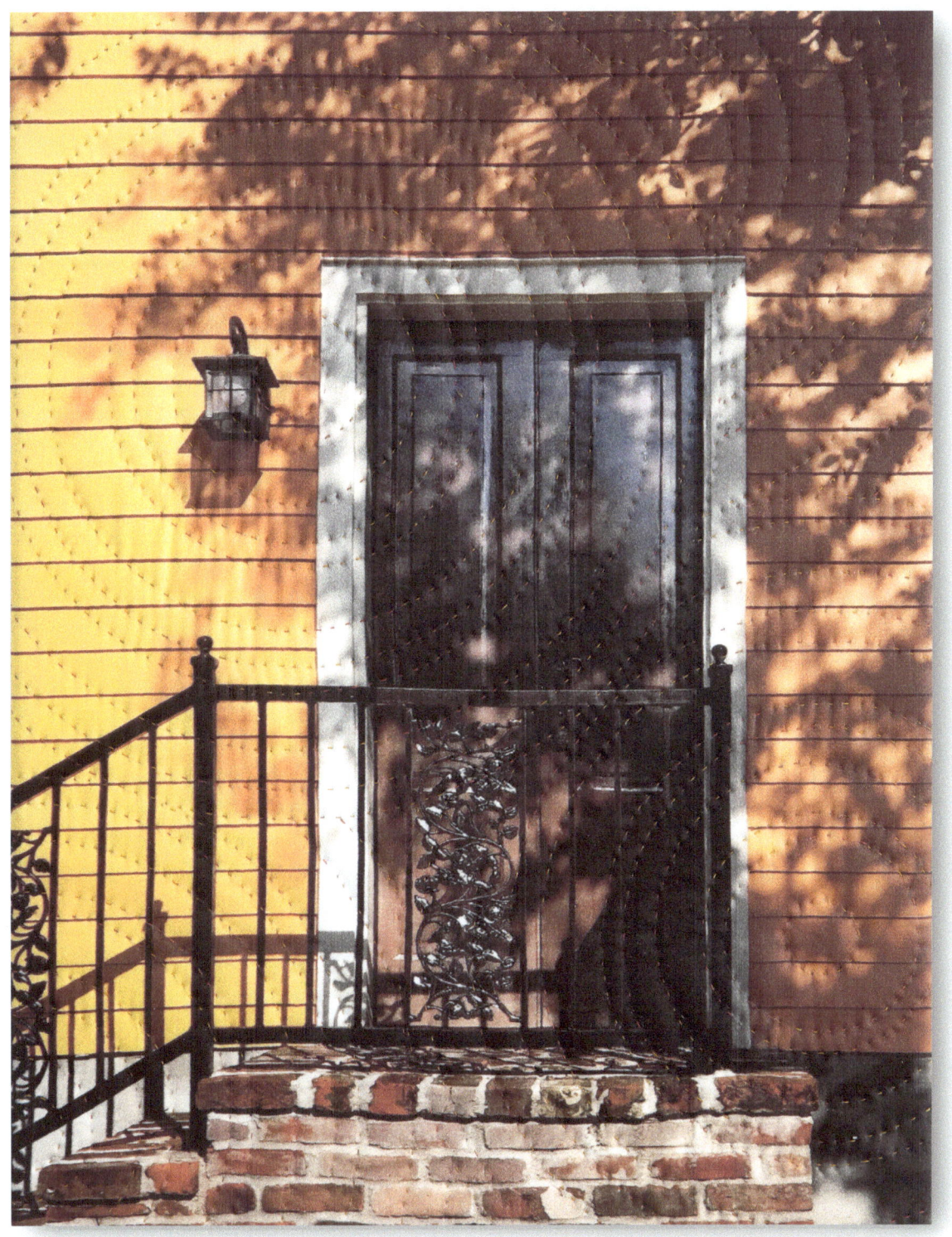

Spain Street   14"x11".   cotton, hand quilted

"Madame Lily Devalier always asked "Where are you?" in a way that insinuated that there were only two places on earth one could be: New Orleans and somewhere ridiculous."

— Tom Robbins, Jitterbug Perfume

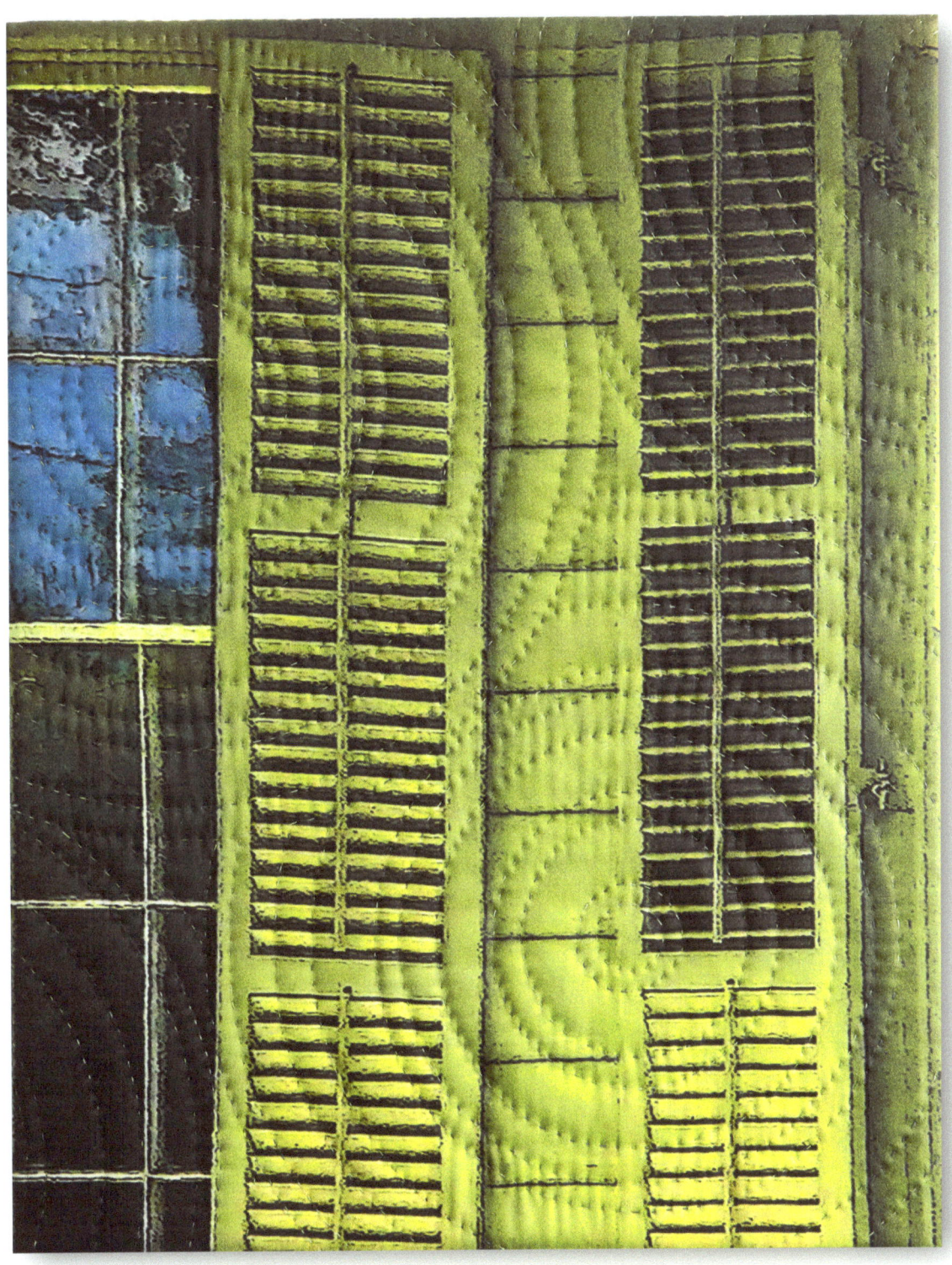

Philip Street 2   14"x11".   cotton, hand quilted

"She had understood before she had ever dreamed of a city such as this, where every texture, every color, leapt out at you, where every fragrance was a drug, and the air itself was something alive and breathing."

— Anne Rice, The Witching Hour

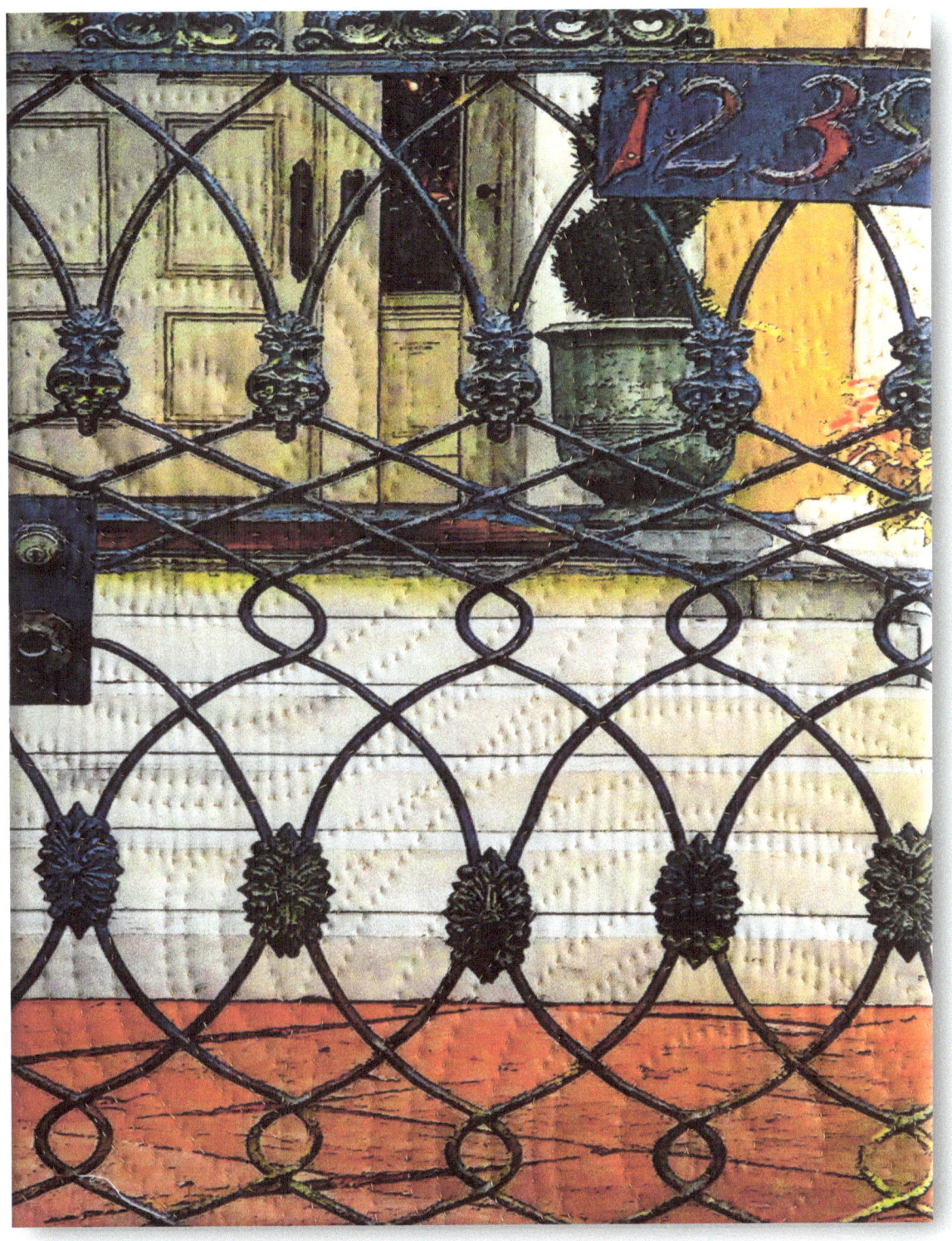

First Street   14"x11".   cotton, hand quilted

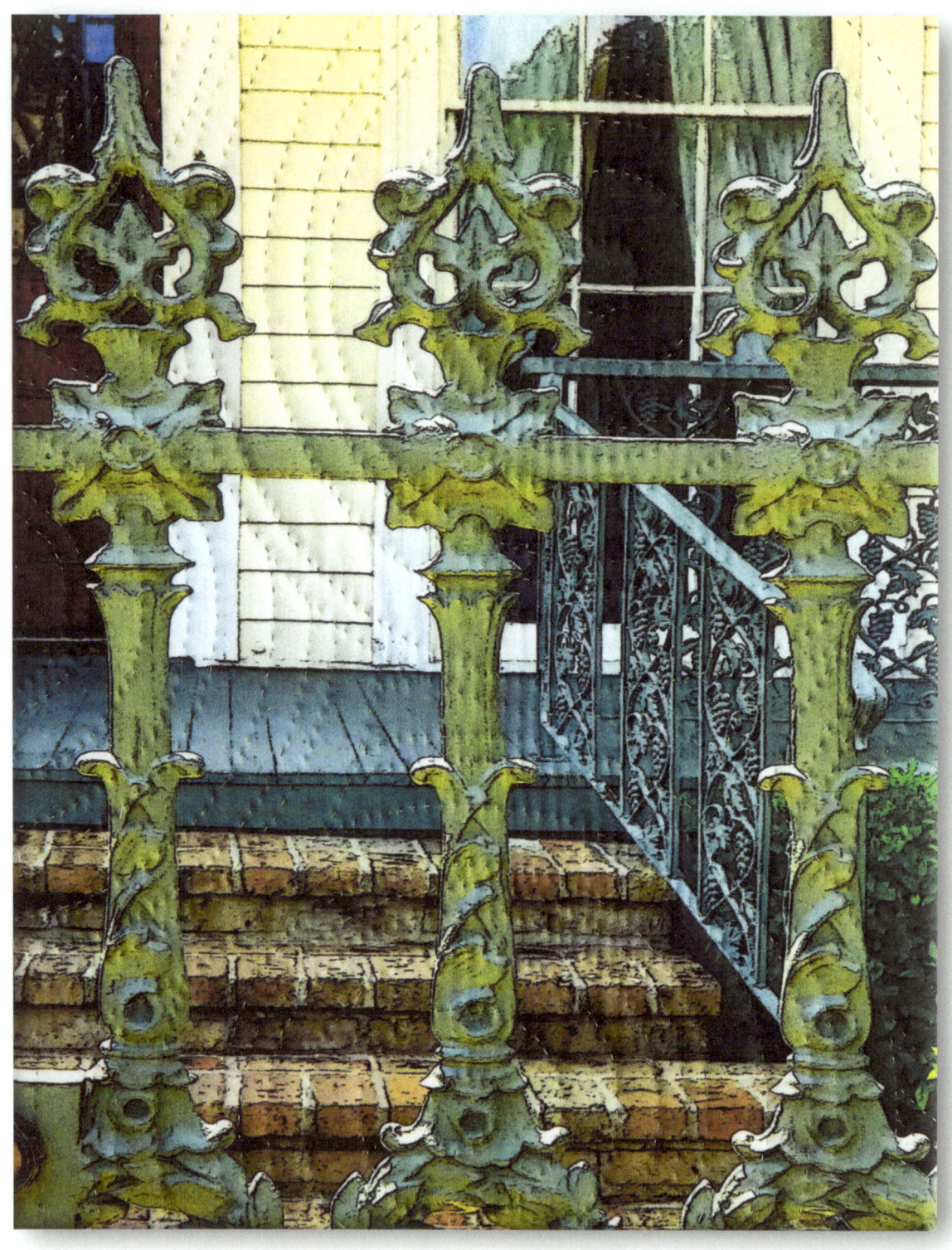

Philip Street 2   14"x11".   cotton, hand quilted

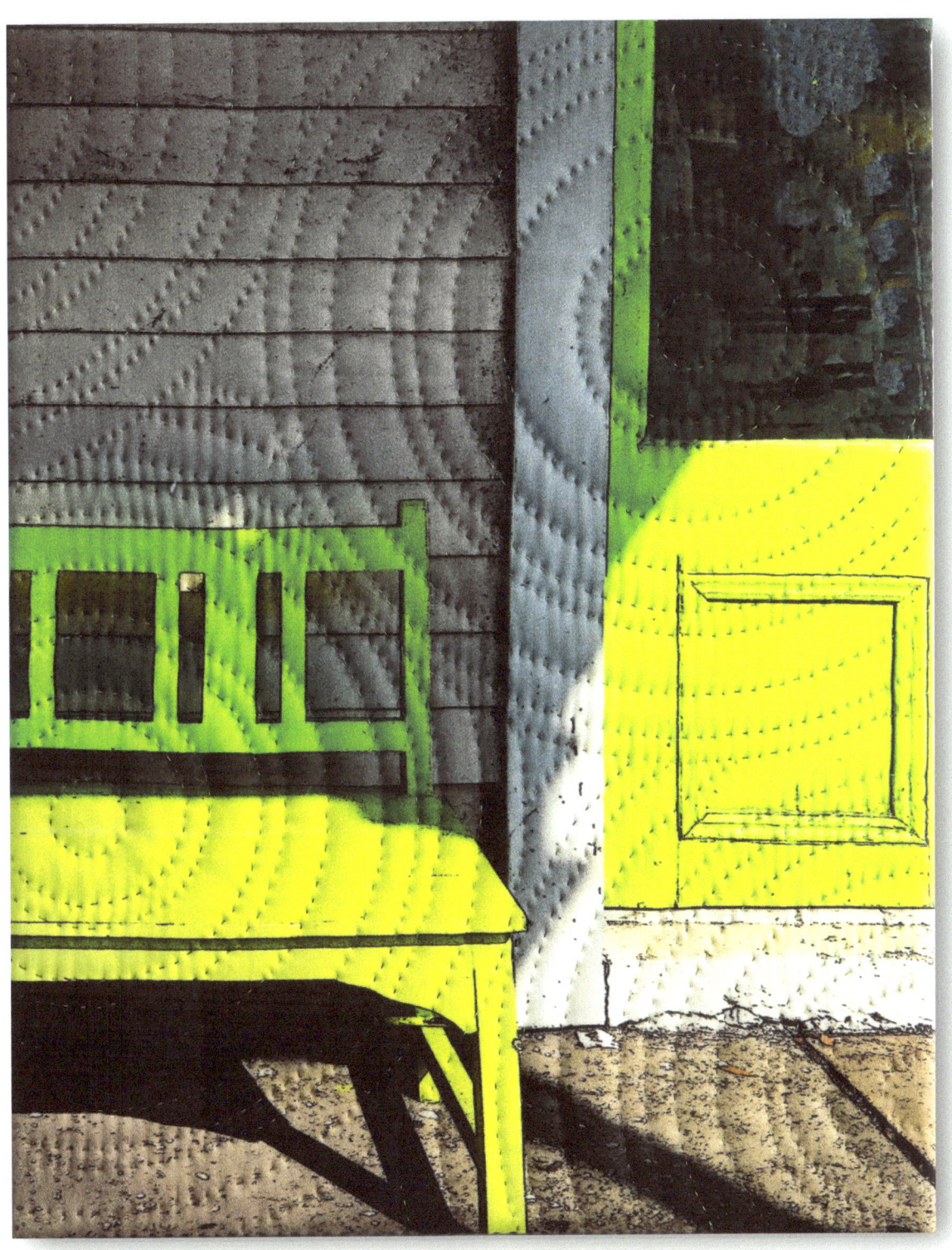

Magazine Street   14"x11".   cotton, hand quilted

"Even the sidewalks in New Orleans had personality."

— Hunter Murphy, Imogene in New Orleans

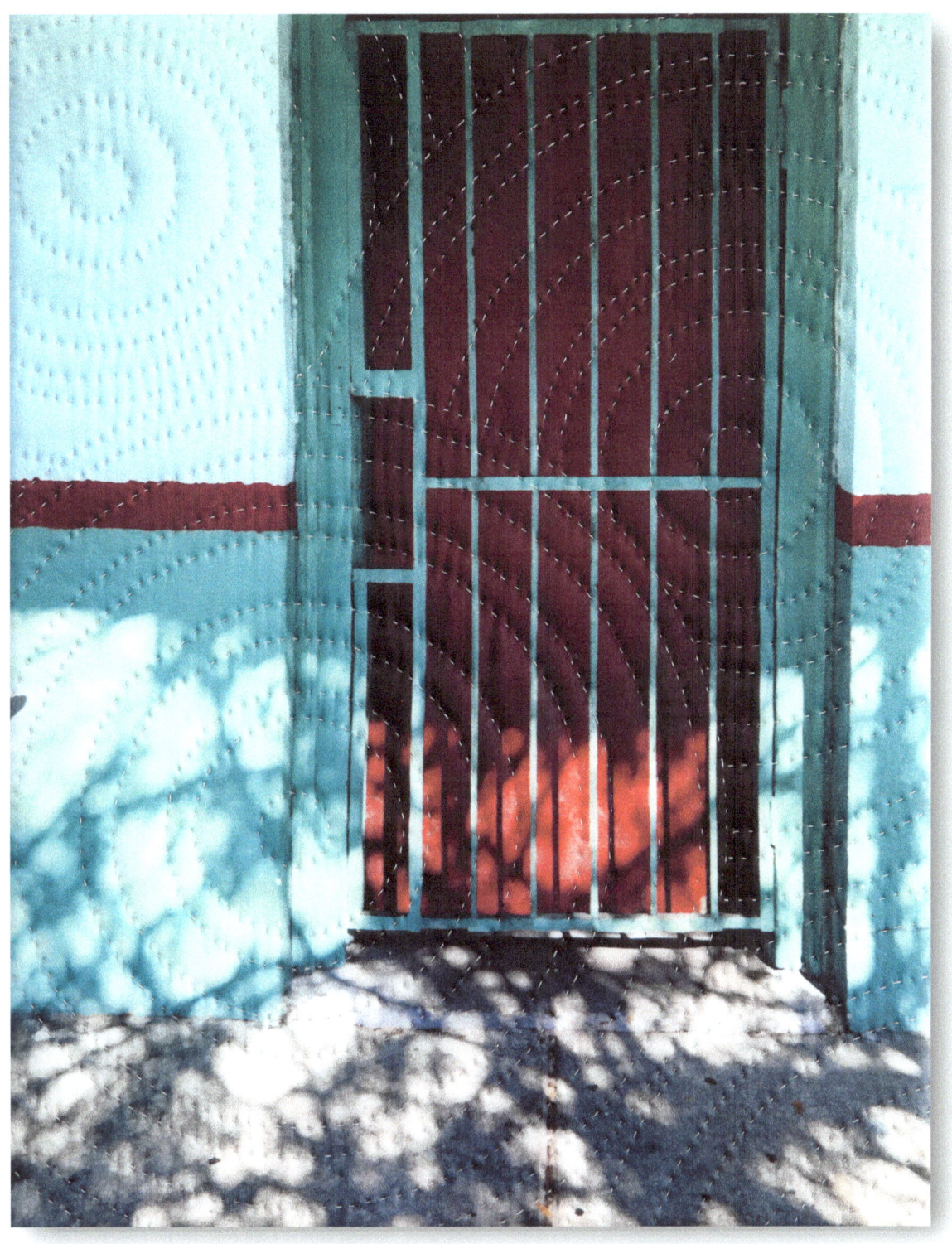

Marigny Street   14"x11".   cotton, hand quilted

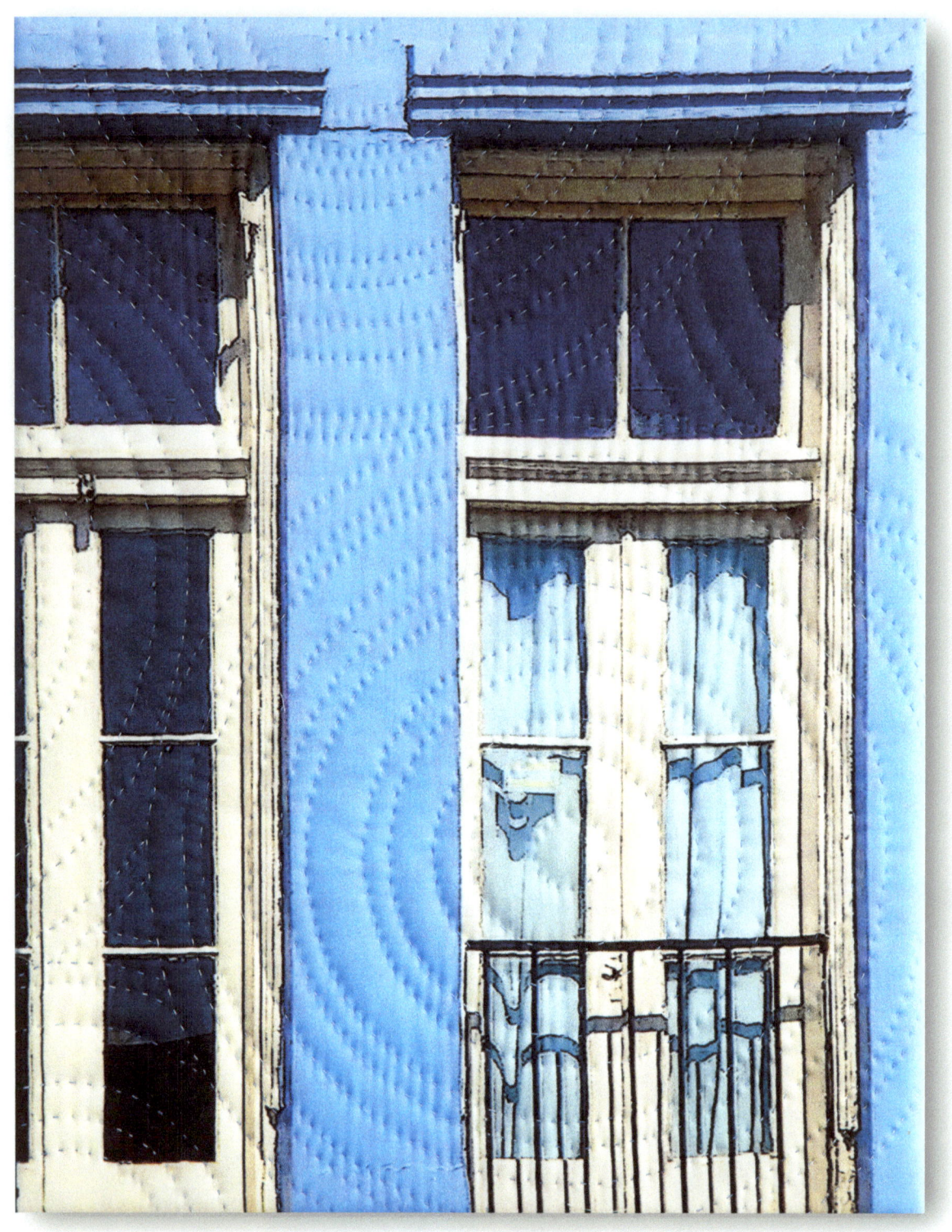

Decatur Street   14"x11".   cotton, hand quilted

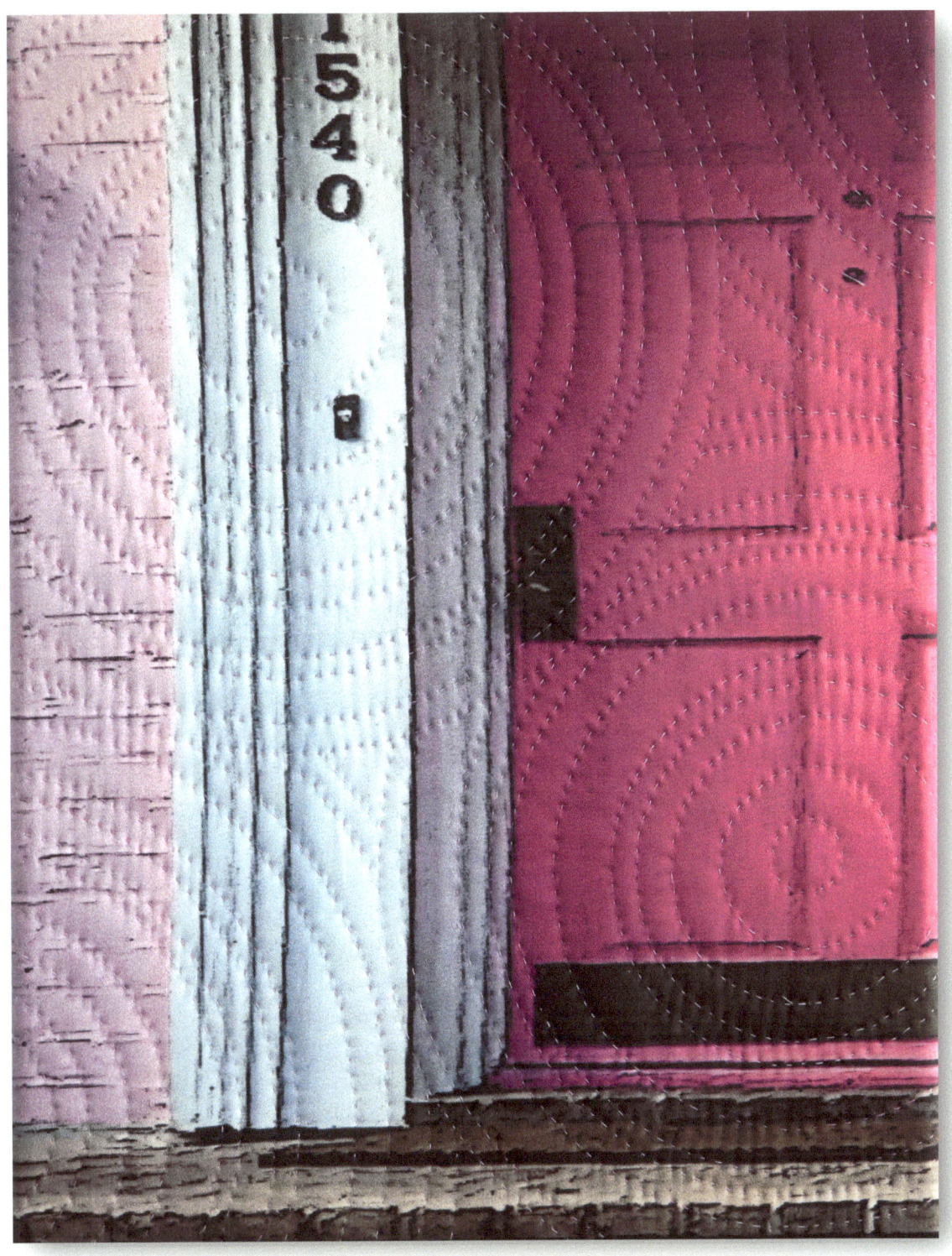

Harmony Street   14"x11".   cotton, hand quilted

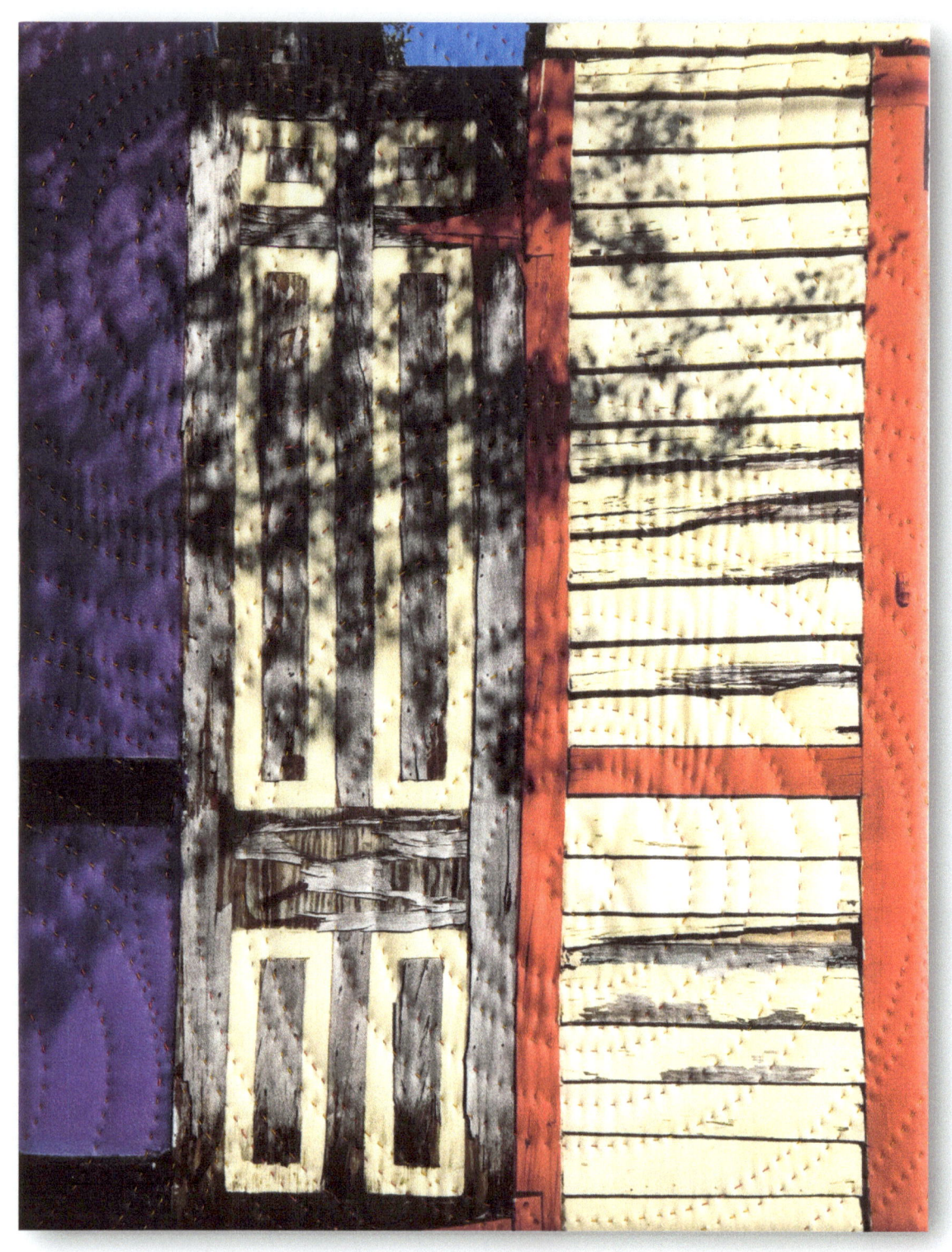

Marigny Street 3   14"x11".   cotton, hand quilted

"If there was no New Orleans, America would just be a bunch of free people dying of boredom." -Judy Deck in an e-mail sent to Chris Rose"

— Chris Rose, 1 Dead in Attic: Post-Katrina Stories

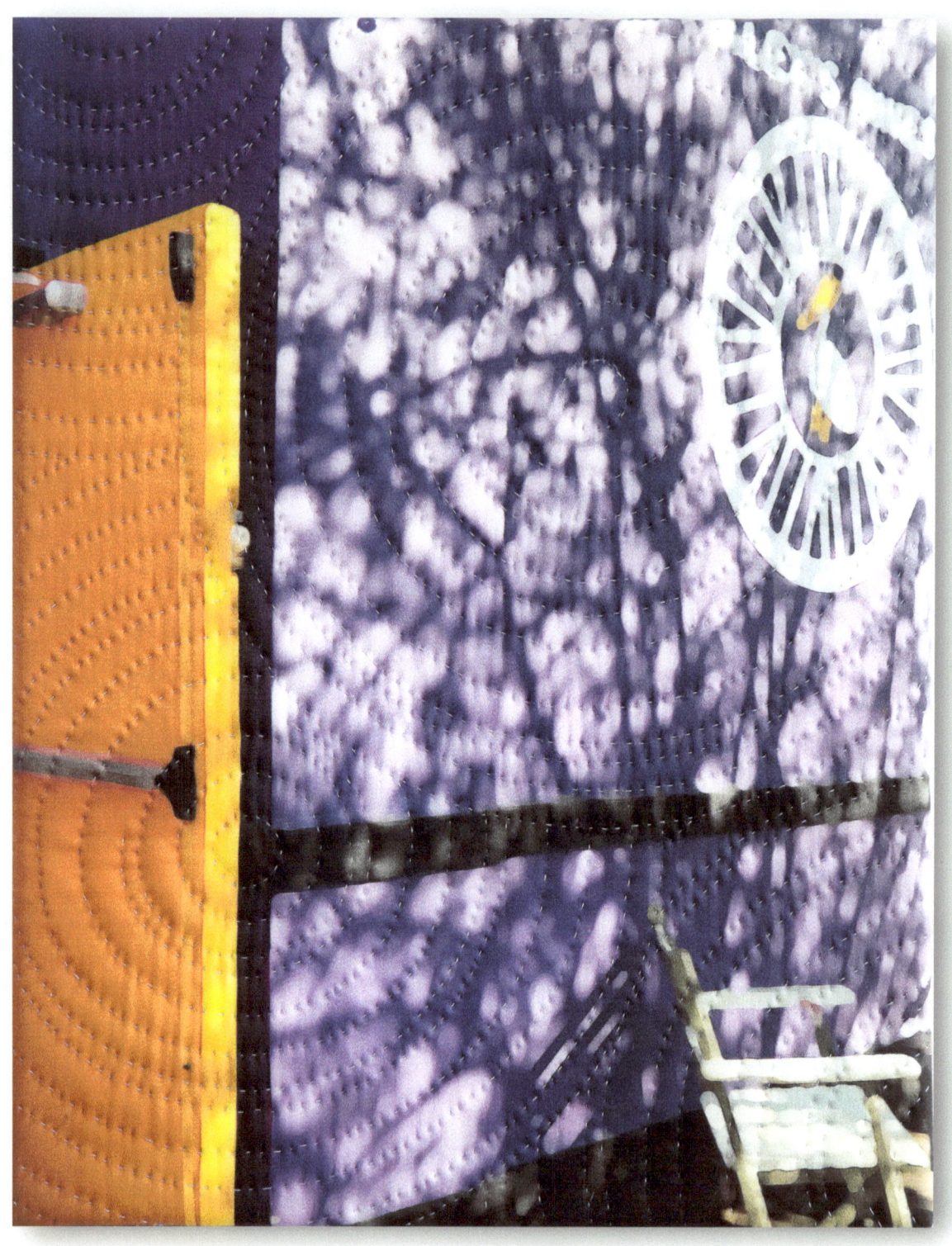

Marigny Street 2   14"x11".   cotton, hand quilted

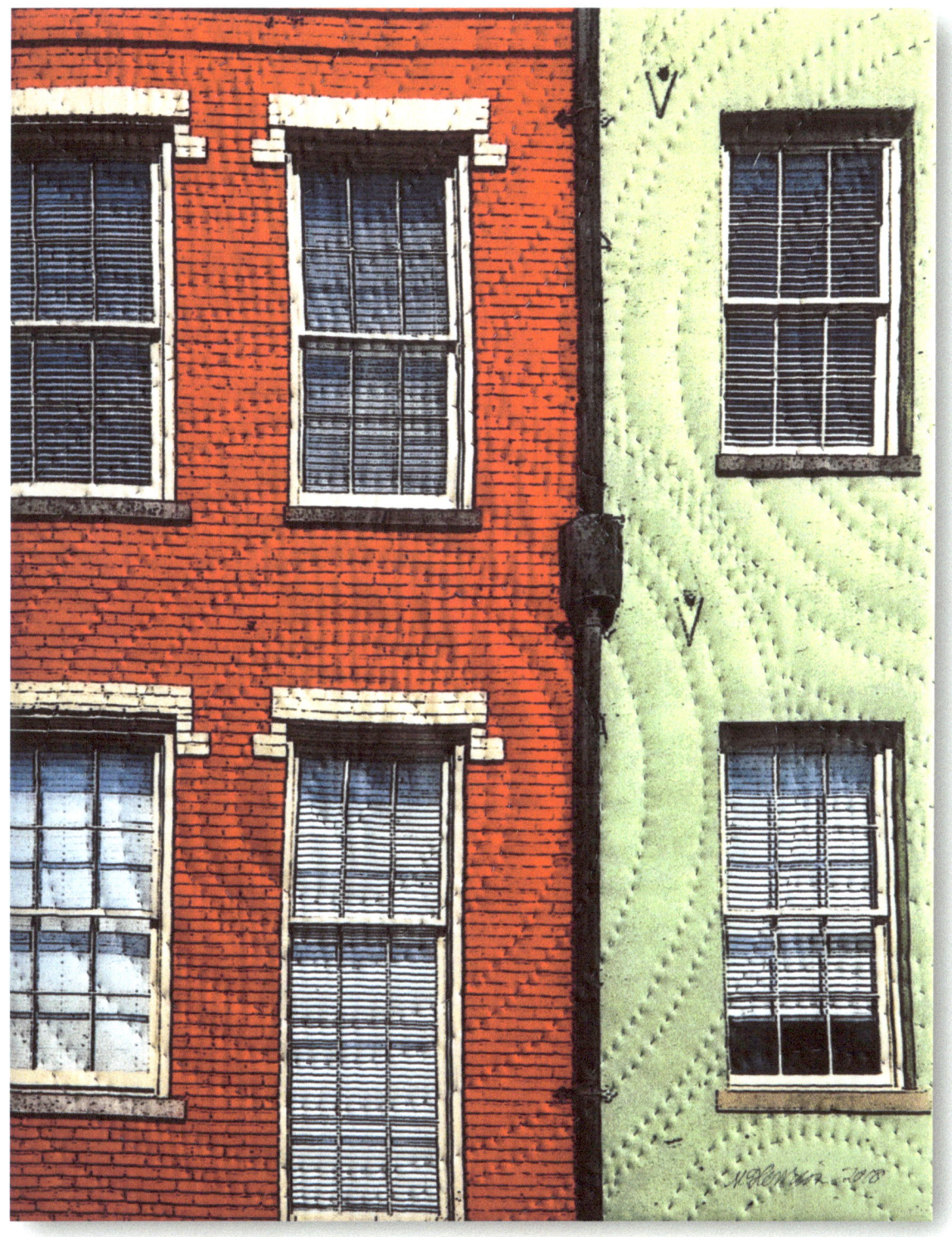

North Peters Street   14"x11".   cotton, hand quilted

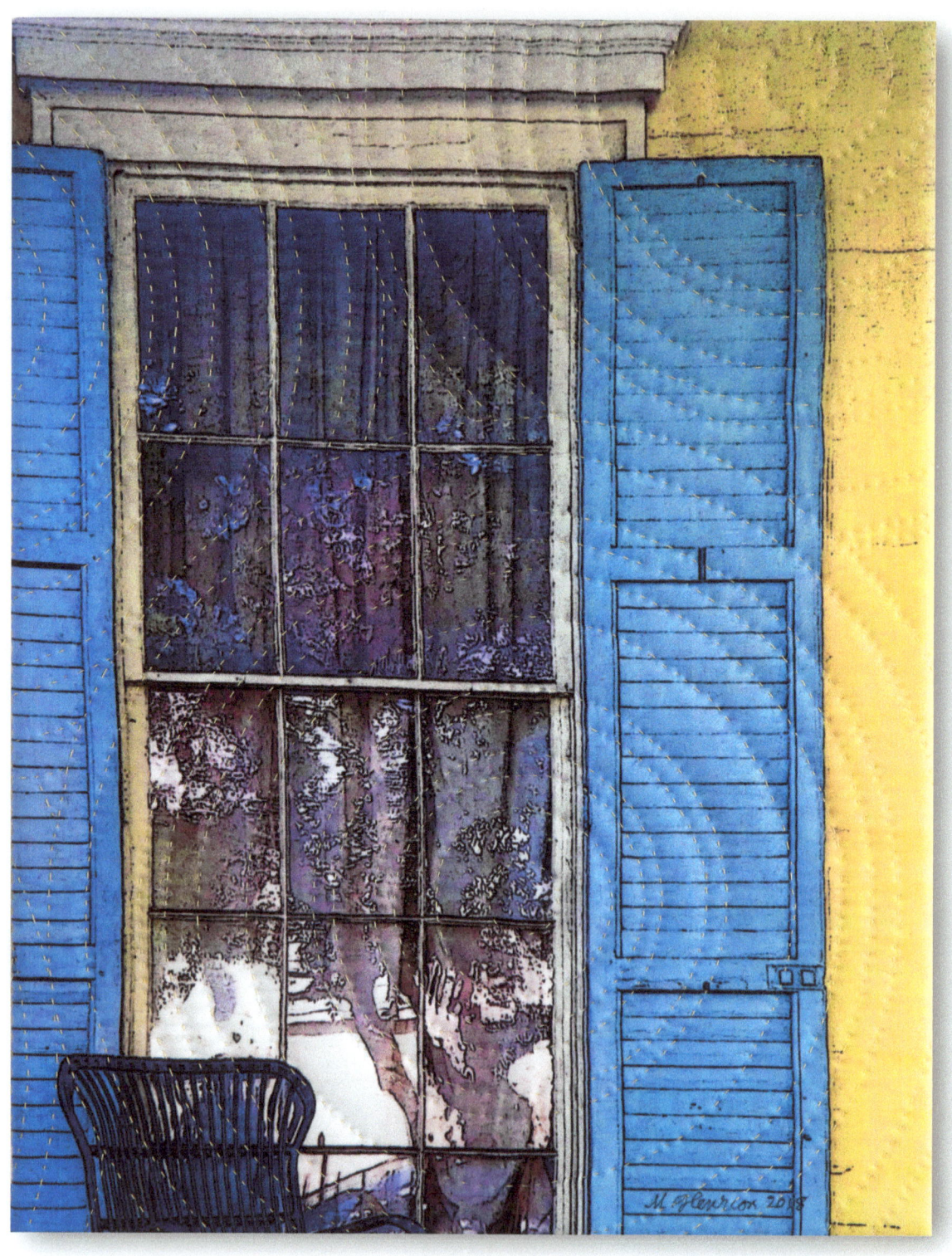

Chestnut Street 2   14"x11".   cotton, hand quilted

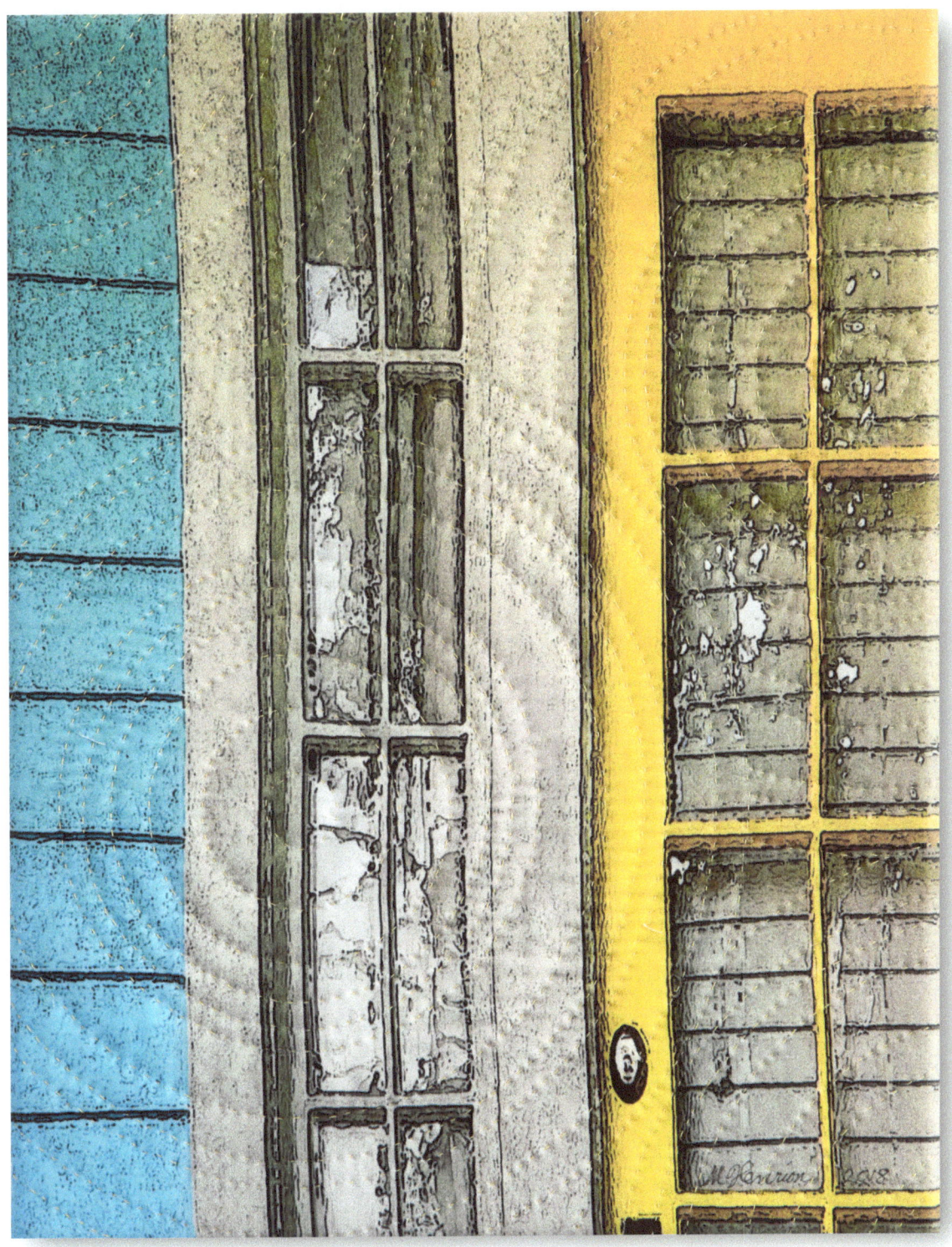

Chestnut Street 3   14"x11".   cotton, hand quilted

"Everything in New Orleans is a good idea. Bijou temple-type cottages and lyric cathedrals side by side. Houses and mansions, structures of wild grace. Italianate, Gothic, Romanesque, Greek Revival standing in a long line in the rain. Roman Catholic art. Sweeping front porches, turrets, cast-iron balconies, colonnades- 30-foot columns, gloriously beautiful- double pitched roofs, all the architecture of the whole wide world...."

— Bob Dylan, Chronicles, Vol. 1, 2004

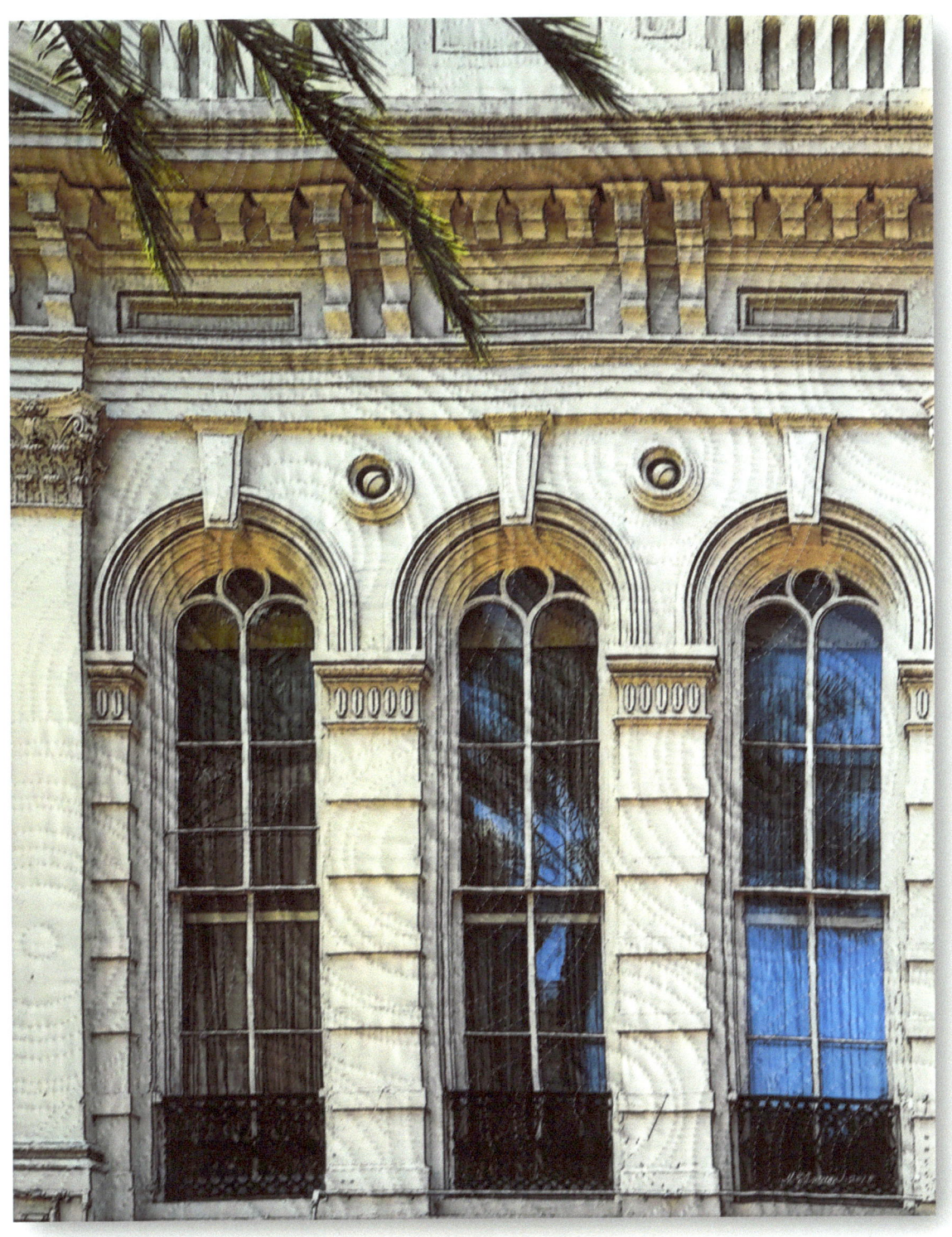

Canal Street   30"x24".   cotton, hand quilted

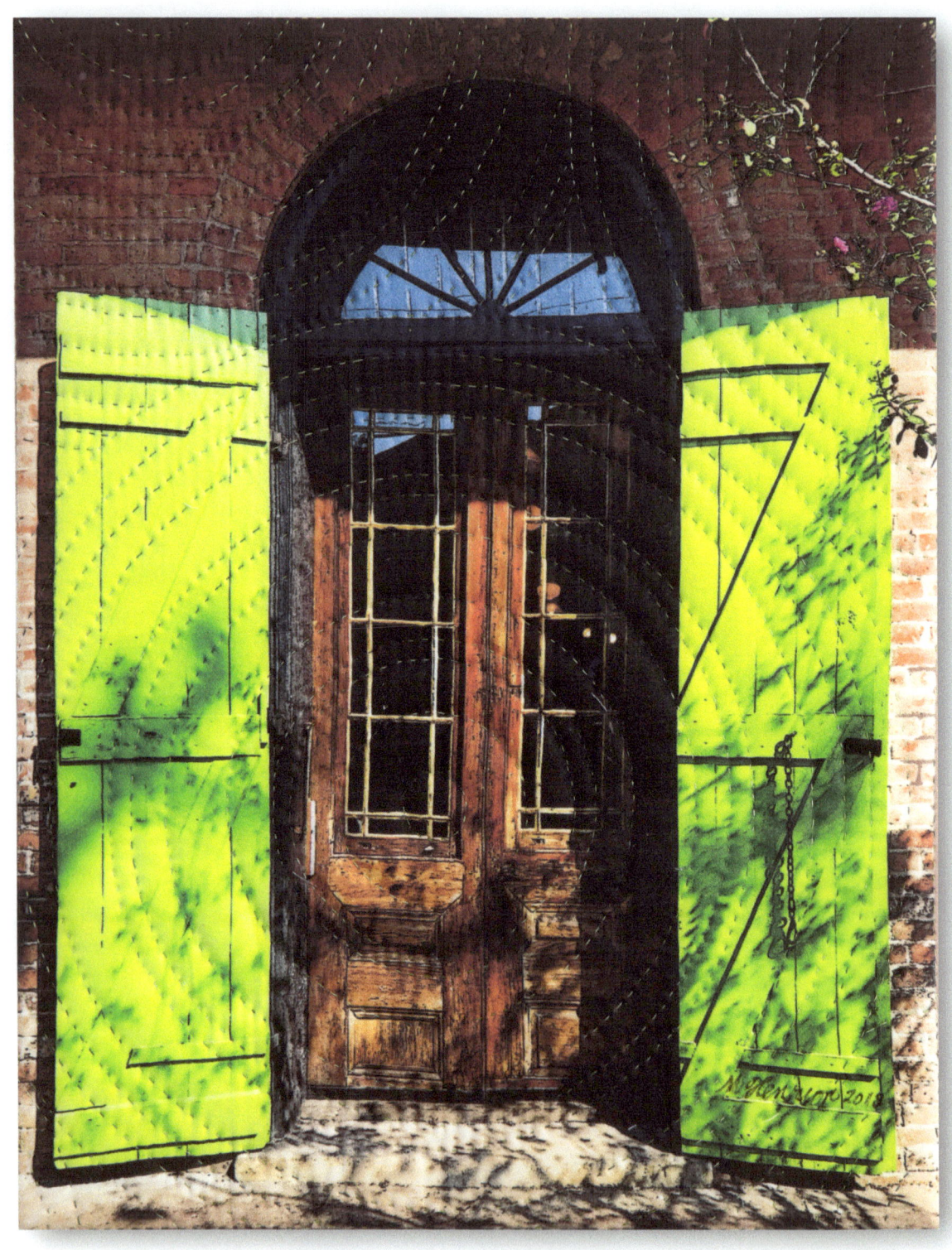

Port Street   14"x11".   cotton, hand quilted

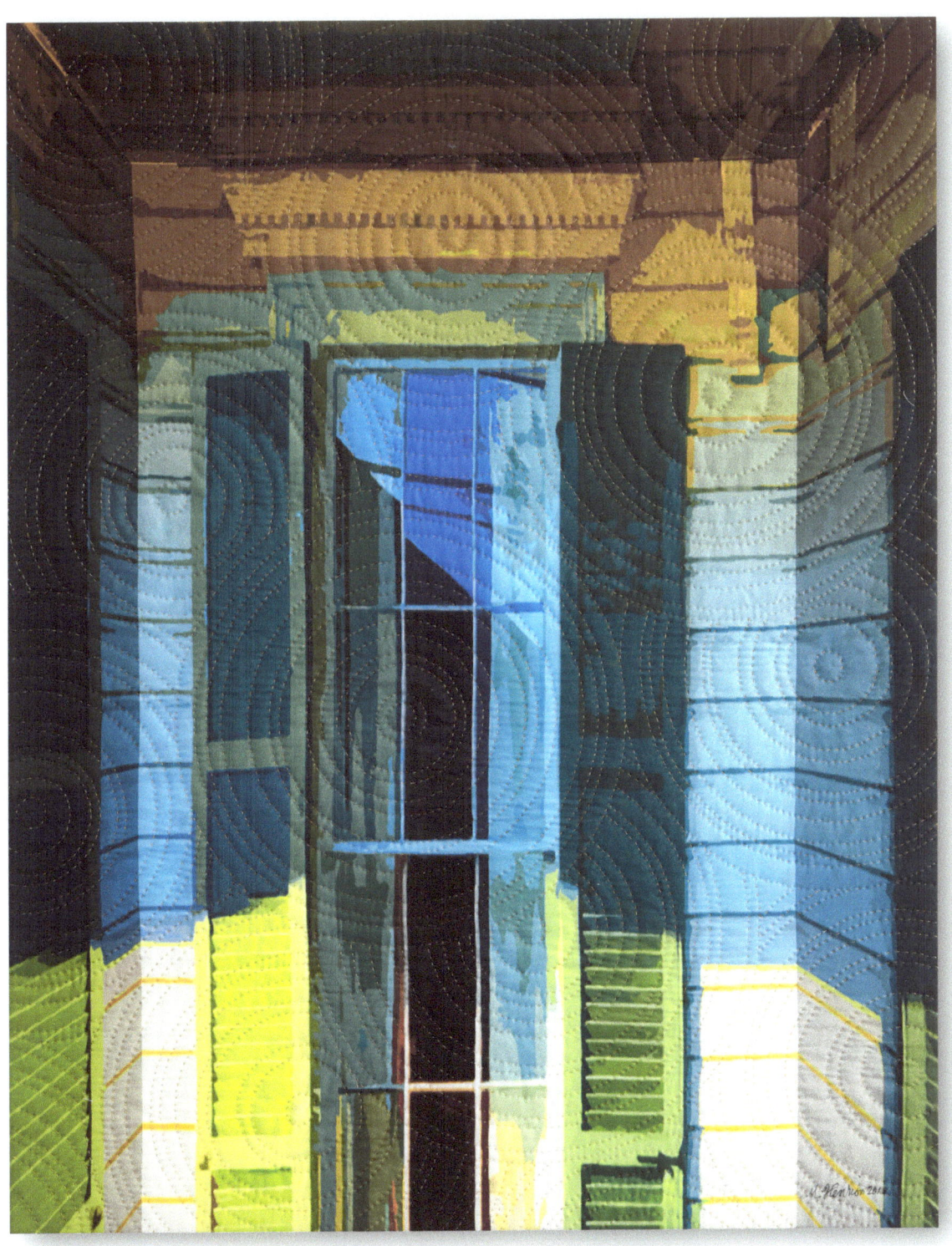

NOLA Fantasy   30"x24".   cotton, hand quilted

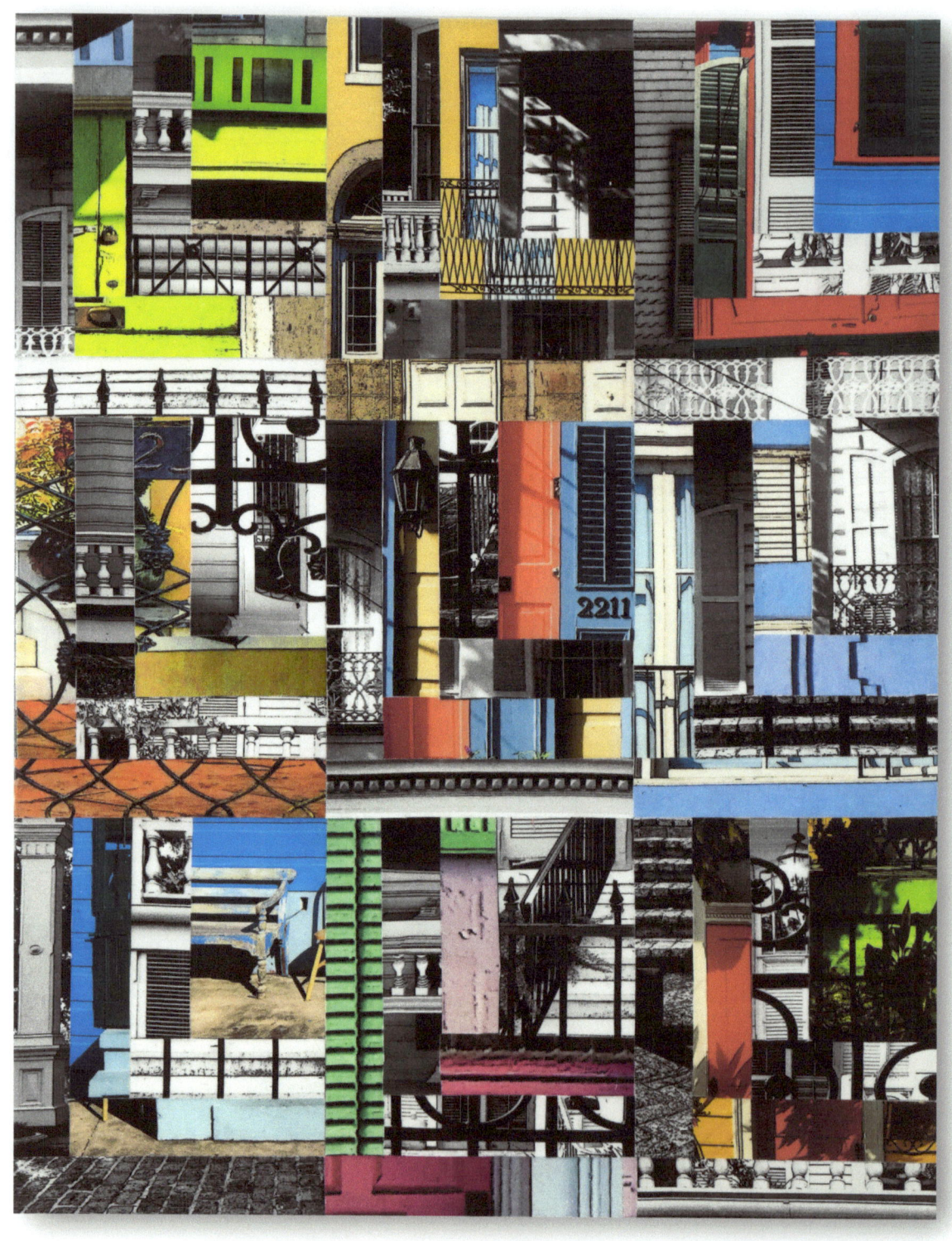

NOLA Gumbo 1   30"x24".   linen collage on canvas

"Not so much as a single pebble 'came' from New Orleans, any more than any of the people did. Every grain of sand, every rock, every drip of brown mud, and every single person walking, living and loving in the city is a refugee from somewhere else. But they made something unique, the people and the land, when they came together in that cohesive, magnetic, magical spot; this sediment of society made something that is not French, not Spanish, and incontrovertibly not American."

— James Caskey, The Haunted History of New Orleans: Ghosts of the French Quarter

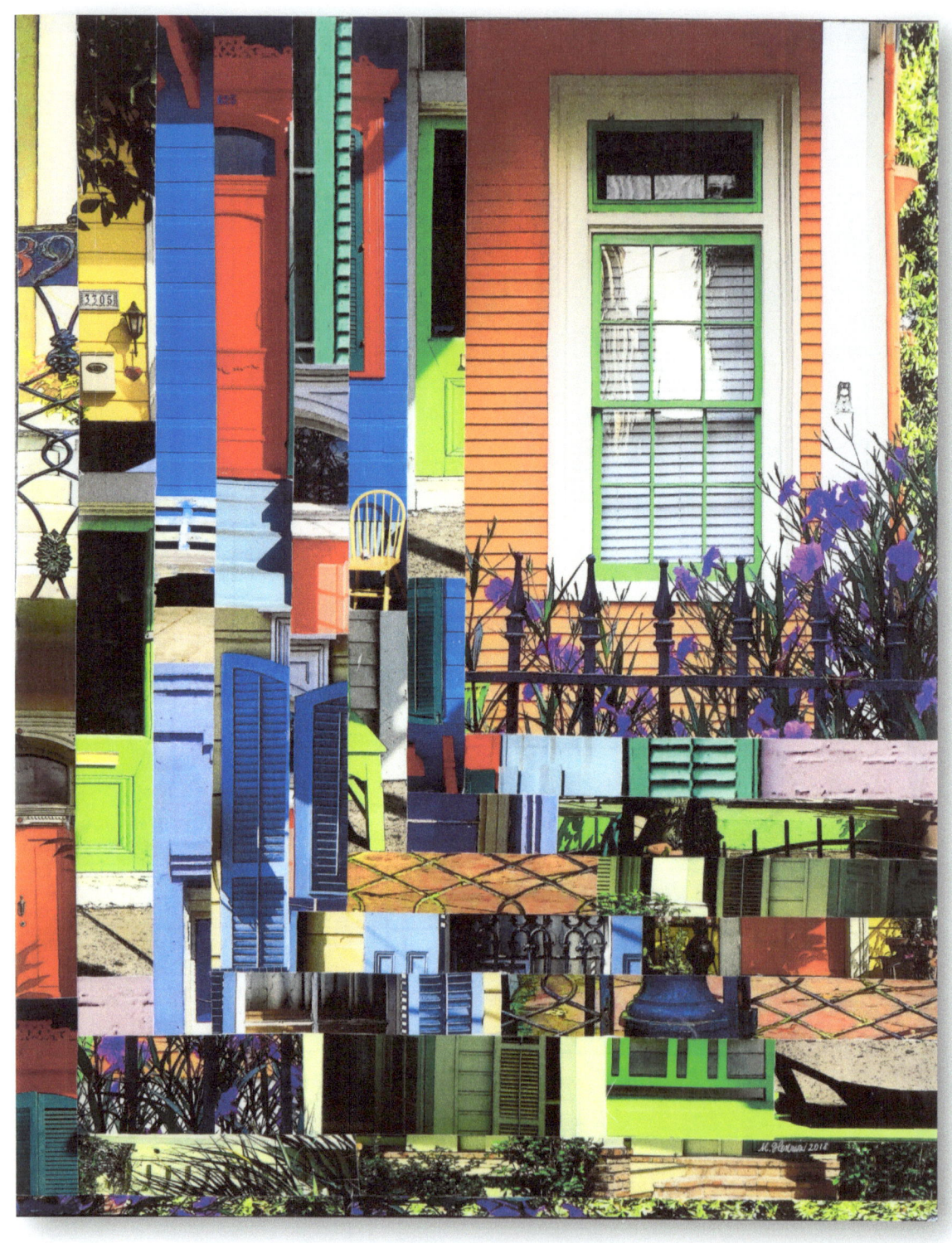

NOLA Gumbo 2   30"x24".   linen collage on canvas

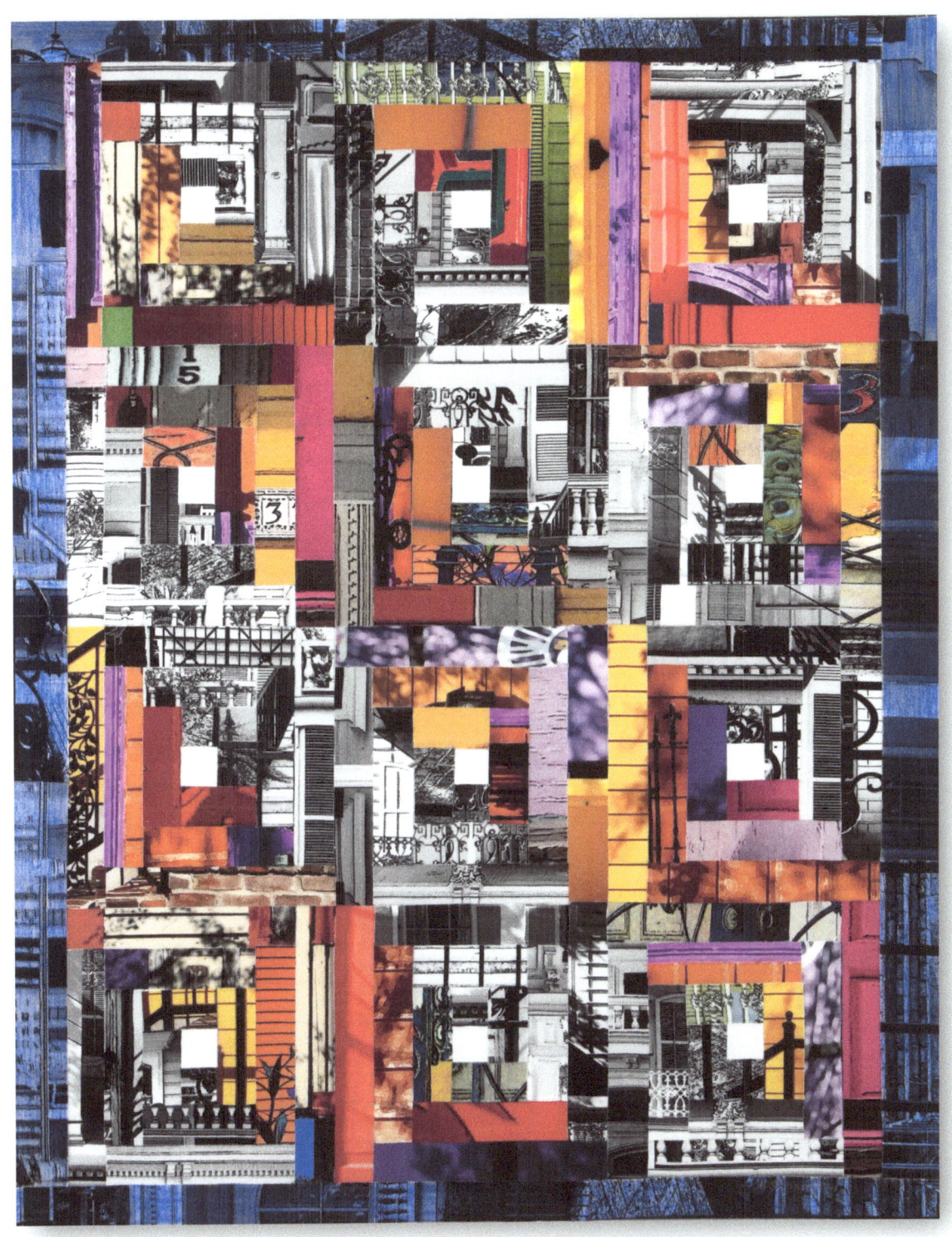

NOLA Gumbo 3   30"x24".   linen collage on canvas

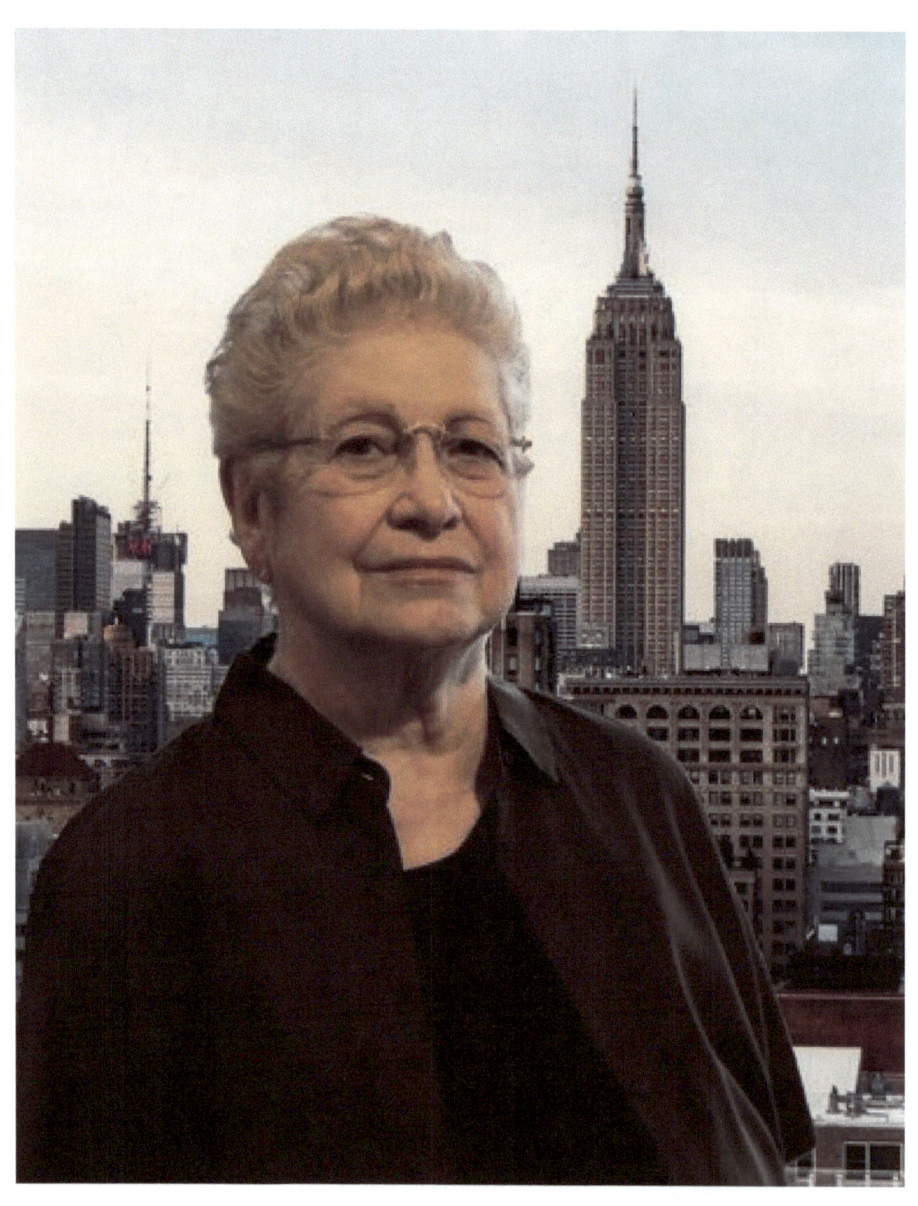

The artist in her studio

BIOGRAPHY

Born in 1932, Marilyn Henrion is a life-long New Yorker and a graduate of Cooper Union. She is represented in the Smithsonian Institution's Archives of American Art. After graduating from Cooper Union in 1952, she married fellow-artist and classmate, Edward Henrion, a marriage that lasted 64 years until his passing in 2016, and which produced four children.

During the 1950's and '60's, Marilyn and Ed were immersed in the art and literary scene of the era, attending meetings at the 8th Street Club where the abstract expressionists gathered, holding poetry salons at their Greenwich Village apartment where the "Beat" poets of the day would read from their work. Marilyn performed in Claes Oldenburg's "Happenings" and at the newly-founded Judson Poets Theatre on Washington Square. Sunday afternoon visits to friend Joseph Cornell and babysitting by Tom and Clare Wesselmann (then students at Cooper Union) were part of their lives.

After retiring from a twenty-year career as Associate Professor/Career Counselor at the Fashion Institute of Technology in 1989, Marilyn was able to devote full time to her creative life. Although she started as a painter in 1952, it was textiles that spoke to her in a way that paint never did. Upon resuming her creative work in the 1970's, textiles became her medium of choice. Initially working in the "art quilt" genre, the labor-intensive process of hand quilting added a meditative quality to the aesthetic challenges of "piecing" a work of art that appealed to her.

Over the years, Marilyn's work has continually evolved, with a new body of work being created for a solo exhibition every two years since 1999. Her works are included in museum, corporate and private collections internationally. The current mixed media works still incorporate the textiles and piecing and hand stitching that characterized her earlier work. As an octogenarian with unflagging energy, the artist still spends most of her time in the studio, creating new works for her next exhibition as well as for site-specific commissions.

SOLO EXHIBITIONS

2017 Noho-M55 Gallery, New York, NY
2015 Noho-M55 Gallery, New York, NY
2013 Noho-M55 Gallery, New York, NY
2013 Durst Lobby Gallery, New York, NY
2012 Noho Gallery. New York, NY
2011 Visions Art Museum, San Diego, CA
     Bayer Corporation, Wayne & Montvale, NJ
     Intermezzo Art Gallery, Bergen Performing Arts Center, Englewood, NJ
2010 Noho Gallery, New York, NY
2009 Bayer Corporation, Wayne & Montvale, NJ
     Berkeley College Art Gallery, New York, NY
2008 Noho Gallery, New York, NY
2006 Noho Gallery, New York, NY
     Galerie Gora, Montreal, Quebec, Canada
2005 Treasure Room Gallery, The Interchurch Center, New York, NY
2004 Noho Gallery, New York, NY
     Studio Decouvrir, Hope, ID
2002 Noho Gallery, New York, NY
2001 Thirteen Moons Gallery, Santa Fe, NM
2000 Noho Gallery, New York, NY
1997 Decouvrir Gallery, Seattle, WA
     La Conner Quilt Museum, La Conner, WA
     Atlantic Community College Art Gallery, Mays Landing, NJ
     Leman Publications Art Gallery, Golden, CO
1996 American Association .for the Advancement of Science, Washington, DC
1994 Merrill Lynch Corporate Headquarters, Plainsboro, NJ
1992 Educational Testing Services Corp., Princeton, NJ

COLLECTIONS

Museum of Arts & Design, New York, NY

Newark Museum, Newark, NJ

Racine Art Museum, Racine, WI

Central Museum of Textiles, Lodz, Poland

International Quilt Museum & Study Center, Lincoln, NE

National Quilt Museum, Paducah, KY

U.S. State Department..U.s. Embassy, Pnom Penh, Cambodia

LinkedIn Corporate Headquarters, New York, NY

Mitsubishi Trust & Bank, New York, NY

Nihon Vogue, Tokyo, Japan

Avaya Communications, Denver, CO

Kaiser Permanente, Denver, CO

Lucent Technologies, Denver, CO

Dana Farber Cancer Institute, Boston, MA

Comanche County Medical Center, Lawton, OK

Carnegie Abbey Country Club, Narragansett, RI

SAS Institute, Cary, NC

Rodale Press, Emmaus, PA

Valley Hospital, Ridgewood, NJ

Santa Rita Medical Center, Lima, OH

+ many private collections internationally including Japan, Lebanon, Austria, Russia, USA

OTHER PUBLICATIONS

Patchwork City*, 2017

WINDOWS, Third Edition*, 2016

WINDOWS, Second Edition, 2014 (out of print)

WINDOWS, First Edition, 2013 (out of print)

Marilyn Henrion: The Evolution of a Fiber Artist (DVD)*, 2013

Complexity*, 2012

Soft City*, 2010

Disturbances*, 2008

Noise*, 2006

Reverberations: Keeping Time*, 2004, reprinted 2014

With Edward Henrion…
Mickey Rat*, 2017

Sweet & Lovely*, 2011

Top Hat*, 2011

Book of Chance I*, 2009

*available on amazon.com

www.ingramcontent.com/pod-product-compliance
Lightning Source LLC
Chambersburg PA
CBHW051222220526
45473CB00003B/1141